# I Remember

## A Collection of Special Recipes from the UBC Bakeshop

UBC FOOD GROUP

UBC Food Group
2071 West Mall
Vancouver, British Columbia
V6T 1Z2

Canadian Cataloguing-in-Publication Data
Main entry under title:
Treats to Remember

Includes index
ISBN 0-88865-366-2

1. Baking. I. Samson, Christine
II. Leong, Allen
III. UBC Food Group

TX765.T73 1995 641.8'65 C95-910630-8

*This book is dedicated to all employees*
*of the UBC Food Group and to all*
*our customers – past, present and future.*

| | |
|---|---|
| Editors: | Christine Samson |
| | Allen Leong |
| Design: | Warren Oneschuk, On Design |
| Illustrations: | Kathy Curry |
| Food Styling: | Becky Paris Turner |
| Photography: | Raymond Lum |
| Printing: | Northburn Printers & Gra**F/X** Ink |

Printed and bound in Canada.
Text pages printed on recycled paper.

# Contents

By Popular Demand .......... vi
The UBC Cinnamon Bun .......... 1
Cakes & Quick Breads .......... 5
Christmas Baking .......... 31
Cookies .......... 49
Desserts .......... 59
Muffins & Scones .......... 81
Pies, Tortes & Flans .......... 99
Squares & Bars .......... 117
Recipe Acknowledgments .......... 135
Index .......... 136

# By Popular Demand!

In 1986, responding to numerous requests from the public for recipes, the UBC Food Group published a book of bakeshop recipes edited by the late Shirley Louie. It was entitled *Favourite Recipes from the UBC Bakeshop.* Little did we know how popular it was to become, with several thousand copies selling out almost immediately and three subsequent reprints.

*Treats to Remember* updates and greatly expands on our previous book. Here you will find many of our classic recipes as well as exciting new creations.

We are proud that so many people associate their fondest university memories with the pastries and desserts produced by our bakeshop. Though the physical surroundings of the campus may change, the aroma of our famous freshly-baked Cinnamon Buns continues to have a magical effect on students, faculty and staff.

We thank all the people, past and present, who have contributed their favourite recipes. They include dieticians, Food Group managers and friends. We also thank Mary Stovell for contributions to the text, Warren Oneschuk for his invaluable guidance and design of this book, Kathy Curry for her illustrations, food stylist Becky Paris Turner and Raymond Lum for photographing the cover. Finally, we gratefully acknowledge all our dedicated and creative bakers for making treats to remember.

Christine Samson

*Christine Samson*

Allen Leong

*Allen Leong*

# The UBC Cinnamon Bun... a Legend in its Time

In 1954, Hungarian baker Grace Hasz perfected the recipe for the UBC Cinnamon Bun. Soon the Faculty Club acknowledged its merits, and production increased from two dozen to three dozen per day.

By 1955, Grace was baking twelve dozen per day and supplying the Bus Stop Coffee Shop as well as the Old Cafeteria. She then moved with the Commissary to the Old Cafeteria kitchen, where business skyrocketed to 120 dozen per day. Grace worked at the present Bakeshop from 1968 until she retired in 1971 at the age of 72.

Today, the Bakeshop produces about 150 dozen per day – and UBC Alumni always list the UBC Cinnamon Bun as one of the top ten memories of university life.

# The UBC Cinnamon Bun

| | | |
|---|---|---|
| 3 cups | milk | 750 mL |
| 6 tbsp | margarine | 90 mL |
| 6 tbsp | sugar | 90 mL |
| 1 tbsp | salt | 15 mL |
| 1 tsp | sugar | 5 mL |
| 1/2 cup | warm water | 125 mL |
| 2 envelopes | active dry yeast | |
| 2 | large eggs | 2 |
| 9 cups | all-purpose flour | 2.25 L |

FILLING

| | | |
|---|---|---|
| 3/4 cup | melted margarine | 175 mL |
| 1 1/4 cups | sugar | 300 mL |
| 2 tbsp | cinnamon | 30 mL |

1. Preheat oven to 350°F (180°C).
2. Scald milk. Stir in margarine, the 6 tbsp (90 mL) sugar and salt. Cool to lukewarm.
3. Dissolve the 1 tsp (5 mL) sugar in warm water. Sprinkle yeast over water mixture. Let stand in warm place for 10 minutes. Stir.
4. In large mixing bowl, combine lukewarm milk mixture and eggs. Stir in dissolved yeast.
5. Add four to five cups (1 to 1 1/4 L) of the flour and beat well for 10 minutes. With wooden spoon, gradually add enough of the remaining flour to make a soft dough.
6. Turn out on to lightly floured surface and knead until smooth and elastic, adding additional flour as needed. (This is a soft dough).

*continued...*

# The UBC Cinnamon Bun

7. Place in well greased bowl and roll dough over to grease the top. Cover with damp cloth and let rise in a warm place until dough doubles in size, about one hour.

8. Punch down and turn out on lightly floured surface. Divide dough in half.

9. To fill, roll out each piece of dough into 9 x 18 inch (23 x 46 cm) rectangle. Spread 1/4 cup of margarine evenly onto each rectangle.

10. Combine sugar and cinnamon. Sprinkle onto the rectangles. Roll dough up like a jelly roll, starting from the long side. Cut into 2 inch slices.

11. Place remaining 1/4 cup of melted margarine in bottom of 16 1/2 x 11 1/2 x 2 1/2 inch (42 x 30 x 6 cm) pan. Arrange slices in pan and cover loosely with greased wax paper.

12. Let rise in pan until doubled in size, about 45 to 60 minutes.

13. Bake at 350°F for 35 to 40 minutes.

14. Remove from oven and immediately invert onto a serving tray.

Makes 18 large cinnamon buns.

**Note:**
The Bakeshop uses fresh yeast which may alter the final product slightly.

# Cakes & Quick Breads

Cakes are the most sociable of pastries. We cannot imagine birthdays or weddings without them. They are also perfect for informal occasions such as coffee with friends. Here we present some favourite UBC cake recipes for your home enjoyment.

# Banana Oatmeal Cake

*Bananas and rolled oats in combination make this cake nutritious and delicious. The boiled topping of brown sugar, nuts and flaked coconut is reminiscent of the Lazy Daisy Cake.*

| | | |
|---|---|---|
| 2 cups | all-purpose flour | 500 mL |
| 1 cup | rolled oats | 250 mL |
| 2 tsp | baking powder | 10 mL |
| 1 tsp | baking soda | 5 mL |
| 1/2 tsp | salt | 2 mL |
| 1/4 tsp | nutmeg | 1 mL |
| 1/2 cup | butter | 125 mL |
| 1 1/4 cup | sugar | 300 mL |
| 2 | eggs | 2 |
| 1 tsp | vanilla | 5 mL |
| 1 1/2 cups | mashed banana | 375 mL |
| 3/4 cup | buttermilk | 175 mL |

**TOPPING**

| | | |
|---|---|---|
| 1/4 cup | butter | 50 mL |
| 3/4 cup | brown sugar | 175 mL |
| 1/3 cup | cream | 75 mL |
| 1 1/2 cups | flaked coconut | 375 mL |
| 2/3 cup | walnuts, chopped | 150 mL |

1. Preheat oven to 350°F (180°C).
2. Combine first 6 ingredients. Mix well.
3. Cream butter, sugar, eggs and vanilla together on medium speed of electric mixer until light and fluffy.
4. Add dry ingredients alternately with banana and buttermilk, mixing lightly after each addition.

*continued...*

## Banana Oatmeal Cake

5. Spread batter evenly on greased 13 x 9 inch (32 x 22 cm) cake pan.

6. Bake for 35 – 40 minutes or until toothpick inserted in centre comes out clean. Cool 10 minutes.

7. Preheat broiler.

**TOPPING**

8. Melt butter in saucepan.

9. Stir in remaining ingredients.

10. Spread evenly over warm cake.

11. BROIL with oven door partially open, approximately 6 inches (15 cm) from heat, for about 2 minutes or until golden brown.

# Blueberry Sour Cream Cake

*Sour cream makes this cake light yet moist. A topping of brown sugar, cinnamon and nuts is the finishing touch.*

| | | |
|---|---|---|
| 1/2 cup | butter | 125 mL |
| 1 cup | sugar | 250 mL |
| 3 | large eggs | 3 |
| 1 cup | sour cream | 250 mL |
| 2 cups | all-purpose flour | 500 mL |
| 1 tsp | baking soda | 5 mL |
| 1/2 tsp | salt | 2 mL |
| 1 tsp | vanilla | 5 mL |
| 2 cups | fresh blueberries, rinsed, drained and floured | 500 mL |
| 1 tbsp | flour | 15 mL |
| TOPPING | | |
| 1/2 cup | firmly packed brown sugar | 125 mL |
| 1/2 cup | chopped nuts | 125 mL |
| 1/2 tsp | cinnamon | 2 mL |

1. Preheat oven to 350°F (180°C).
2. In a bowl, cream butter until light and fluffy.
3. Beat in sugar. Beat in eggs, one at a time, beating until smooth after each addition.
4. Stir in sour cream. Stir in flour, baking soda, salt and vanilla. Beat until smooth and well blended.

*continued...*

## Blueberry Sour Cream Cake

5. Toss blueberries in the one tbsp (15 mL) flour and fold into batter.

6. Spread the batter into a greased 9 x 13 inch (3.5 L) pan.

7. In a bowl, mix brown sugar, nuts and cinnamon. Sprinkle mixture evenly over top of batter in pan.

8. Bake for 40 to 45 minutes.

9. Cool in pan and then cut into squares to serve. Serve sprinkled with icing sugar.

# Blueberry Yogurt Pound Cake

*A moist and buttery cake filled with the flavour and aroma of blueberries and orange. Serve as a coffee cake warm from the oven.*

| | | |
|---|---|---|
| **1 cup** | **butter** | **250 mL** |
| **1 1/3 cups** | **sugar** | **325 mL** |
| **3** | **eggs** | **3** |
| **3 cups** | **all-purpose flour** | **750 mL** |
| **1 1/2 tsp** | **baking soda** | **7 mL** |
| **1/2 tsp** | **salt** | **2 mL** |
| **2 cups** | **blueberries** | **500 mL** |
| **1 cup** | **yogurt** | **1** |
| **3/4 cup** | **orange juice** | **175 mL** |
| **1 tbsp** | **grated orange rind** | **15 mL** |
| | **icing sugar** | |

1. Preheat oven to 350°F (180°C).
2. In large bowl, cream butter until fluffy.
3. Beat in sugar until mixture is light and fluffy, 5 to 8 minutes.
4. Beat in eggs one at a time.
5. Stir or sift together flour, baking soda and salt; mix in berries.
6. In separate bowl, stir together yogurt, orange juice and rind.
7. Mix 1/3 of the dry ingredients into batter; add half of the yogurt mixture.

*continued...*

# Blueberry Yogurt Pound Cake

8. Stir in another third of the dry ingredients, then remaining yogurt mixture and dry ingredients.

9. Pour into well-greased and floured deep 9 or 10 inch (3 L) tube or bundt pan; smooth top and tap pan lightly on work surface to remove air bubbles.

10. Bake for 60 to 70 minutes or until tester inserted in centre comes out clean and cake is well-risen. Let cool for 15 minutes.

11. Dust with icing sugar.

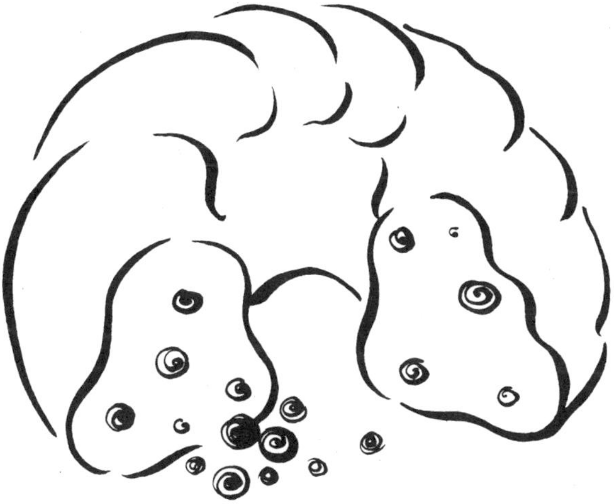

# Crumb Cake

*This spicy, crumb-topped coffee cake is best when served warm.*

| | | |
|---|---|---|
| 1 1/2 cups | packed brown sugar | 375 mL |
| 1 1/2 cups | all-purpose flour | 375 mL |
| 2 tsp | cinnamon | 10 mL |
| 1 tsp | nutmeg | 5 mL |
| 1/2 tsp | cloves | 2 mL |
| 1/2 tsp | salt | 2 mL |
| 1/2 cup | butter | 125 mL |
| 1 tsp | baking powder | 5 mL |
| 1/2 tsp | baking soda | 2 mL |
| 1 | egg, beaten | 1 |
| 2/3 cup | buttermilk | 150 mL |
| 1 cup | raisins | 250 mL |

1. Preheat oven to 350°F (180°C).
2. Combine brown sugar, flour, cinnamon, nutmeg, cloves and salt.
3. With pastry blender or 2 knives, cut in butter until mixture resembles fine crumbs; set aside 3/4 cup (175 mL).
4. To remaining crumbs, add baking powder and baking soda. Stir in beaten egg, buttermilk and raisins.
5. Pour batter into greased 8 inch square (20 cm) baking pan and top with reserved crumbs.
6. Bake for 40 minutes or until tester inserted in centre comes out clean.

# Glazed Lemon Bread

*This simple loaf can be served with fruit for dessert or just sliced and served with tea or coffee.*

**CAKE**

| | | |
|---|---|---|
| 2 cups | all-purpose flour | 500 mL |
| 3 tsp | baking powder | 15 mL |
| 1/2 tsp | salt | 2 mL |
| 1 cup | sugar | 250 mL |
| 1/3 cup | melted butter | 75 mL |
| 2 | eggs, lightly beaten | 1 |
| 1 cup | milk | 250 mL |
| | grated peel of 1/2 lemon | |
| 1/2 tsp | vanilla | 2 mL |

**GLAZE**

| | | |
|---|---|---|
| 2 tbsp | sugar | 250 mL |
| 2 tbsp | lemon juice | 30 mL |

1. Preheat oven to 350°F (180°C). Lightly grease a 9 x 5 inch (22 x 12 cm) loaf pan.
2. Combine flour, baking powder, salt and sugar.
3. In a separate bowl, combine remaining ingredients.
4. Add the liquid ingredients all at once to dry ingredients. Stir just until moistened.
5. Turn into prepared pan and bake for 60 – 65 minutes, or until toothpick inserted in centre comes out clean.
6. Remove cake from pan and cool on rack.
7. When almost cool, top with lemon glaze.

**GLAZE**

8. Combine sugar and lemon juice and mix until sugar is dissolved. Spoon mixture over top of cake.

# Never Fail Chocolate Cake

*At UBC, this cake is filled with strawberries and whipped cream and iced with a rich chocolate icing. You may also use cherries and kirsch to make a version of Black Forest Cake and frost with whipped cream.*

| | | |
|---|---|---|
| 2 | eggs | 2 |
| 2 cups | buttermilk or sour milk | 500 mL |
| 1/2 cup | vegetable oil | 125 mL |
| 1 tsp | vanilla | 5 mL |
| 3/4 cup | cocoa powder | 175 mL |
| 1 3/4 cups | flour | 425 mL |
| 2 cups | sugar | 500 mL |
| 1 tsp | baking powder | 5 mL |
| 1 tsp | baking soda | 5 mL |

1. Preheat oven to 350°F (180°C).
2. In a blender mix together eggs, milk, oil, vanilla and cocoa.
3. In another bowl combine flour, sugar, baking powder and baking soda.
4. Whisk the liquid into the dry ingredients and pour into two 9 inch (22 cm) round prepared cake pans.
5. Bake for 25 minutes or until toothpick comes out clean. Cool before filling and frosting.

# Ponderosa Cake

*This is the most popular cake and most sought after recipe at UBC.*

| | | |
|---|---|---|
| 1 cup | butter | 250 mL |
| 2 cups | sugar | 500 mL |
| 2 | eggs, beaten | 2 |
| 1 tsp | vanilla | 5 mL |
| 3 | medium ripe bananas | 3 |
| 3 cups | flour | 750 mL |
| 2 tsp | baking powder | 10 mL |
| 2 tsp | baking soda | 10 mL |
| 1 cup | sour cream | 250 mL |
| 1 tsp | cinnamon | 5 mL |
| 1/2 cup | brown sugar | 125 mL |
| 1 1/2 cups | chocolate chips | 375 mL |

1. Preheat oven to 350°F (180°C).
2. Cream together butter and sugar.
3. Add beaten eggs and beat until smooth.
4. Add vanilla and bananas; mix until smooth.
5. Sift flour, baking powder and baking soda, add to banana mixture alternately with sour cream, ending with dry ingredients.
6. Pour half the batter into greased 9 x 13 inch (22 x 32 cm) pan.
7. Combine cinnamon and brown sugar. Sprinkle half of this mixture over the batter in pan. Top with half of the chocolate chips.
8. Repeat layers.
9. Bake for 45 to 50 minutes.

# Traditional Banana Bread

*This classic recipe is best when made with very ripe bananas.*

| | | |
|---|---|---|
| 2 1/2 cups | all-purpose flour | 625 mL |
| 3 tsp | baking powder | 15 mL |
| 1/2 tsp | baking soda | 2 mL |
| 1/2 tsp | salt | 2 mL |
| 1/2 cup | shortening | 125 mL |
| 1 cup | sugar | 250 mL |
| 3 | eggs, well beaten | 3 |
| 1 1/3 cups | mashed bananas | 325 mL |
| 3/4 cup | chopped walnuts | 175 mL |

1. Preheat oven to 350°F (180°C).
2. Sift together flour, baking powder, baking soda and salt.
3. Blend shortening and sugar until creamy.
4. Beat in eggs and mashed bananas.
5. Add dry ingredients to banana mixture in 3 parts. Beat batter after each addition until smooth.
6. Fold in chopped nuts.
7. Place mixture in a greased loaf pan.
8. Bake about 1 hour or until done. Cool before slicing.

# Spicy Banana Raisin Bread

*This recipe can be made in a bundt pan and iced with a rich cream cheese frosting for special occasions or it can be made in loaf pans and served as the spicier cousin of traditional banana bread.*

| | | |
|---|---|---|
| 1 1/2 cups | sugar | 375 mL |
| 3 | eggs | 3 |
| 3/4 cup | oil | 175 mL |
| 2 cups | all-purpose flour | 500 mL |
| 2 tsp | baking soda | 10 mL |
| 1/2 tsp | salt | 2 mL |
| 1 tsp | cinnamon | 5 mL |
| 1 tsp | allspice | 5 mL |
| 2 cups | mashed bananas | 500 mL |
| 1/2 cup | raisins | 125 mL |

1. Preheat oven to 350°F (180°C). Grease and flour a bundt pan or two 8 x 4 x 3 inch (20 x 10 x 8 cm) loaf pans.

2. Beat sugar and eggs until creamy. Mix in oil.

3. Sift flour, baking soda, salt, cinnamon and allspice. Add to creamed mixture. Mix in bananas and raisins.

4. Pour into pan and bake for 1 hour or until done. Turn out of pan when cool.

# Pumpkin Walnut Bread

*For Halloween or anytime, this loaf has all the flavour of pumpkin pie.*

| | | |
|---|---|---|
| 1 1/2 cups | sifted all-purpose flour | 375 mL |
| 1 tsp | baking powder | 5 mL |
| 1 tsp | baking soda | 5 mL |
| 1/2 tsp | salt | 2 mL |
| 1 tsp | cinnamon | 5 mL |
| 1/2 tsp | ground cloves | 2 mL |
| 3/4 tsp | ground ginger | 3 mL |
| 1/2 tsp | nutmeg | 2 mL |
| 2 | eggs | 2 |
| 3/4 cup | sugar | 175 mL |
| 1/4 cup | golden corn syrup | 50 mL |
| 1/2 cup | corn oil | 125 mL |
| 1 cup | canned pumpkin | 250 mL |
| 1/2 cup | raisins | 125 mL |
| 1/2 cup | chopped walnuts | 125 mL |
| **GLAZE** | | |
| 1/2 cup | golden corn syrup | 125 mL |
| 1/4 cup | water | 50 mL |

1. Preheat oven to 325°F (160°C). Oil and line bottom of a 9 x 5 inch (22 x 12 cm) loaf pan with waxed paper.
2. Sift together the first 8 ingredients. Set aside.
3. Beat eggs until light.
4. Add sugar, syrup, oil and pumpkin and beat until thoroughly combined.
5. Make a well in the dry ingredients; add liquid ingredients all at once and stir until well mixed.

*continued...*

# Pumpkin Walnut Bread

6. Add raisins and nuts and combine well.

7. Pour batter into prepared loaf pan and bake for 80 minutes or until cake tester inserted in centre of cake comes out clean.

8. Remove cake from pan after 10 minutes, peel off waxed paper and cool completely on cake rack.

9. Wrap closely to store. Loaf will slice more easily if stored at least 8 hours. If desired, glaze before serving.

**GLAZE**

10. Combine syrup and water. Bring to a rolling boil.

11. Spread over loaf.

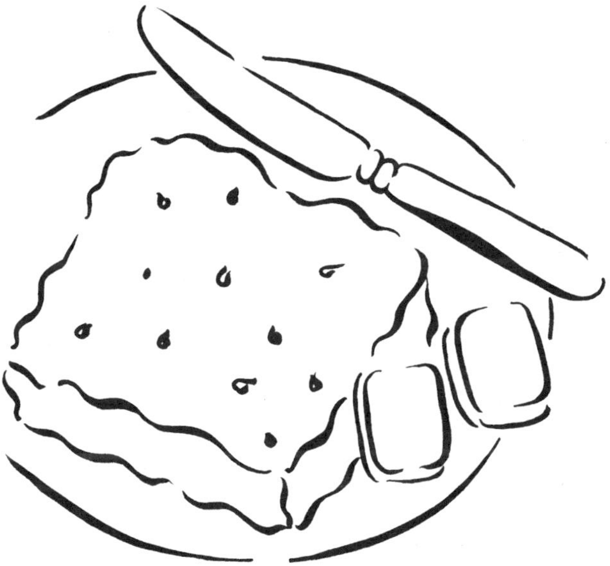

# Over-the-Moon Rhubarb Cake

*For rhubarb lovers this recipe is sure to become a favourite. It can be enjoyed on its own, with coffee, or as dessert topped with whipped cream or ice cream.*

| | | |
|---|---|---|
| **BATTER** | | |
| **1/2 cup** | **butter** | **125 mL** |
| **1 1/2 cups** | **sugar** | **375 mL** |
| **1** | **egg** | **1** |
| **1 tsp** | **vanilla** | **5 mL** |
| **2 cups** | **sifted all-purpose flour** | **500 mL** |
| **1 tsp** | **baking soda** | **5 mL** |
| **1/2 tsp** | **salt** | **2 mL** |
| **1 cup** | **buttermilk** | **250 mL** |
| **2 cups** | **chopped rhubarb in 1/2 inch (1 cm) pieces** | **500 mL** |
| **1 tbsp** | **flour** | **15 mL** |
| **TOPPING** | | |
| **1/4 cup** | **butter** | **50 mL** |
| **2 tsp** | **cinnamon** | **10 mL** |
| **1 cup** | **firmly packed brown sugar** | **250 mL** |

**1.** Preheat oven to 350°F (180°C). Butter bottom of a 13 x 9 inch (3.5 L) cake pan.

**BATTER**

**2.** Cream butter and sugar until smooth and creamy. Beat in egg and vanilla.

**3.** Sift together 2 cups (500 mL) flour, baking soda and salt. Add to creamed mixture alternately with buttermilk.

*continued...*

## Over-the-Moon Rhubarb Cake

**4.** Toss rhubarb with 1 tbsp (15 mL) flour and mix gently into the batter.

**5.** Spoon into the pan and smooth the surface.

**TOPPING**

**6.** Blend together all ingredients and sprinkle evenly over the batter.

**7.** Bake for 45 minutes or until the cake has risen and browned and comes away from the edges. Check that a skewer inserted in the centre comes out clean.

# Almond Brickle

*Something a little different and extra special for almond lovers.*

| | | |
|---|---|---|
| **BASE** | | |
| 1/2 cup | butter | 125 mL |
| 2/3 cup | sugar | 150 mL |
| 2 | eggs | 2 |
| 1 3/4 cups | sifted all-purpose flour | 425 mL |
| 2 tsp | baking powder | 10 mL |
| 1 tsp | almond extract | 5 mL |
| 1/3 cup | milk | 75 mL |
| **TOPPING** | | |
| 1/2 cup | butter | 125 mL |
| 1/3 cup | sugar | 175 mL |
| 1/4 cup | honey | 50 mL |
| 1 tbsp | milk | 15 mL |
| 1/2 cup | slivered, blanched almonds | 125 mL |

1. Preheat oven to 350°F (180°C). Grease a 12 x 8 inch (30 x 20 cm) pan.
2. Combine all topping ingredients in a saucepan. Cook over low heat, stirring constantly until golden brown, about 15 minutes. Cool.
3. Combine all base ingredients in a large mixer bowl and blend well. Beat 3 minutes at medium speed.
4. Pour batter into the pan.
5. Spread with topping.
6. Bake at 350°F (180°C) for 25 to 30 minutes.

# Sour Cream and Cinnamon Coffee Cake

*A classic recipe which is always well received.*

| | | |
|---|---|---|
| 6 tbsp | soft butter | 90 mL |
| 1 cup | sugar | 250 mL |
| 2 | eggs (room temperature) | 2 |
| 1 1/3 cups | flour | 325 mL |
| 1 1/2 tsp | baking powder | 7 mL |
| 1 tsp | baking soda | 5 mL |
| 1 cup | sour cream | 250 mL |
| 2 tbsp | sugar | 30 mL |
| 2 tsp | cinnamon | 10 mL |

1. Preheat oven to 350°F (180°C).
2. Beat butter, sugar and eggs in bowl for 10 minutes.
3. Sift dry ingredients and blend into sour cream.
4. Blend both mixtures together by hand, mixing well.
5. Pour half of batter into greased and floured 9 x 13 inch (22 x 32 cm) pan.
6. Combine the cinnamon and sugar and sprinkle 1 tbsp (15 mL) over the batter.
7. Repeat layers.
8. Bake for 35 minutes or until done.
9. Cool in pan on wire rack and keep at room temperature.

# Cranberry Orange Streusel Coffee Cake

*Now grown in abundance in farm bogs, cranberries are no longer relegated to canned sauces and juice. They combine wonderfully with orange rind in this recipe.*

**STREUSEL**

| | | |
|---|---|---|
| 1/2 cup | packed brown sugar | 175 mL |
| 1/4 cup | all-purpose flour | 50 mL |
| 1/2 tsp | cinnamon | 2 mL |
| 2 tbsp | butter | 15 mL |

**CAKE**

| | | |
|---|---|---|
| 1/2 cup | butter | 125 mL |
| 1 cup | sugar | 250 mL |
| 2 | eggs | 2 |
| 1 tsp | vanilla | 5 mL |
| 2 cups | all-purpose flour | 500 mL |
| 1 tsp | baking powder | 5 mL |
| 1 tsp | baking soda | 5 mL |
| 1/2 tsp | salt | 2 mL |
| 1 cup | sour cream | 250 mL |
| 1 tbsp | grated orange rind | 15 mL |
| 2 cups | cranberries | 500 mL |

1. Preheat oven to 350°F (180°C).

**STREUSEL**

2. Stir together sugar, flour and cinnamon; cut in butter until mixture is crumbly.

**CAKE**

3. In large mixing bowl, cream butter; add sugar and beat until light and fluffy.

4. Stir in eggs, one at a time. Stir in vanilla and beat until well blended.

*continued...*

## Cranberry Orange Streusel Coffee Cake

5. Sift or stir together flour, baking powder, baking soda and salt.

6. Add flour mixture to creamed mixture alternately with sour cream, making 3 additions of each. Stir in orange rind and cranberries.

7. Spread the batter in greased and floured 9 inch (22cm) springform or 9 x 13 inch (22 x 32 cm) pan.

8. Sprinkle with streusel mixture.

9. Bake for about 1 hour and 15 minutes or until tester inserted in centre comes out clean.

10. Let cool in pan for 10 minutes. Remove sides and serve warm. Makes 8 to 10 servings.

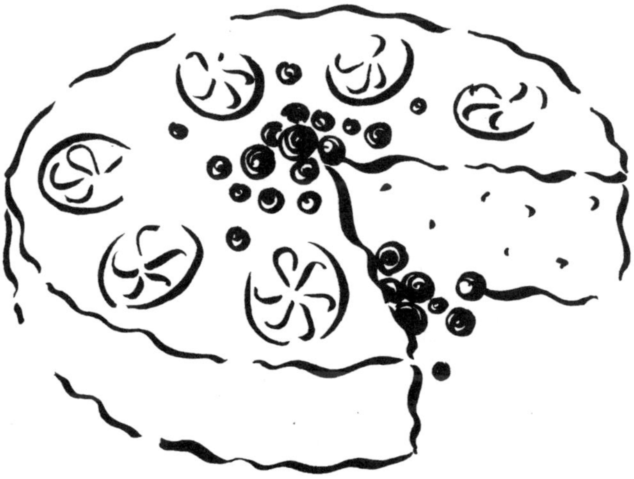

# Fresh Strawberry Coffee Cake

*This showy coffee cake "guilds the lily" by topping delicious sliced strawberries with a sweet, buttery coconut mixture.*

| | | |
|---|---|---|
| **TOPPING** | | |
| 1/2 cup | all-purpose flour | 125 mL |
| 1/2 cup | sugar | 125 mL |
| 1/4 cup | chilled butter | 50 mL |
| 1/4 cup | flaked or shredded coconut | 50 mL |
| **CAKE** | | |
| 3/4 cup | sugar | 175 mL |
| 1/4 cup | soft shortening | 50 mL |
| 1 | medium egg | 1 |
| 1/2 cup | milk | 125 mL |
| 1 tsp | almond extract | 5 mL |
| 1 1/2 cups | sifted all-purpose flour | 375 mL |
| 2 tsp | baking powder | 10 mL |
| 1/2 tsp | salt | 2 mL |
| 1 1/2 cups | sliced fresh strawberries | 375 mL |

**1.** Preheat oven to 375°F (190°C).

**TOPPING**

**2.** Combine flour and sugar.

**3.** Cut in chilled butter and mix in coconut.

**CAKE**

**4.** Mix sugar, shortening and egg thoroughly.

**5.** Stir in milk and almond extract.

*continued...*

# Fresh Strawberry Coffee Cake

6. Sift together flour, baking powder and salt.
7. Stir dry ingredients into shortening mixture.
8. Turn into greased and floured 9 inch (23 cm) square pan.
9. Top with fresh strawberries and sprinkle with coconut topping.
10. Bake for 25 to 35 minutes.

# UBC Coffee Cake

*Developed in the UBC Bakeshop, it has proven its popularity in campus coffee shops and cafeterias for many years.*

**TOP & BASE**

| | | |
|---|---|---|
| 1/2 cup | butter | 125 mL |
| 1 cup | brown sugar | 250 mL |
| 1/2 cup | ground walnuts | 125 mL |
| 1/2 cup | coconut, fine | 125 mL |
| 1/2 tsp | salt | 2 mL |
| 1 cup | pastry flour | 250 mL |

**FILLING**

| | | |
|---|---|---|
| 1/2 cup | butter | 125 mL |
| 1 cup | sugar | 250 mL |
| 2 | eggs | 2 |
| 1/2 tsp | vanilla | 2 mL |
| 1 1/2 cups | pastry flour | 375 mL |
| 1 tsp | baking soda | 5 mL |
| 1/2 tsp | salt | 2 mL |
| 1 1/2 tsp | baking powder | 7 mL |
| 1 cup | sour cream | 250 mL |

1. Preheat oven to 350°F (180°C).

**TOP & BASE**

2. Cream butter and brown sugar well.
3. Add nuts, salt, coconut and flour; mix until crumbly.
4. Press lightly into greased 9 x 13 inch (22 x 32 cm) pans, saving some of the mixture for the top.

**FILLING**

5. Cream butter and sugar well.
6. Add eggs slowly, cream again, add sour cream and vanilla.
7. Sift dry ingredients and add to mixture. Mix until blended.
8. Spread on top of base. Cover with rest of topping.
9. Bake for 30 minutes or until done.

# Trekkers Gingerbread

*This old-fashioned recipe comes from Nova Scotia and is served on campus at Trekkers Restaurant.*

| | | |
|---|---|---|
| 1 | egg | 1 |
| 1/2 cup | sugar | 125 mL |
| 1/2 cup | shortening | 125 mL |
| 1 cup | molasses | 250 mL |
| 2 1/2 cups | flour | 625 mL |
| 2 tsp | baking soda | 10 mL |
| 1/2 tsp | salt | 2 mL |
| 1/2 tsp | cloves | 2 mL |
| 1 tsp | each of cinnamon, ginger, mixed spice and allspice | 5 mL |

1. Preheat oven to 350°F (180°C).
2. Mix together the egg, sugar, shortening and molasses.
3. In a separate bowl, mix together the flour, baking soda, salt and spices. Add to the wet mixture and combine.
4. Add one cup of boiling water to the batter and mix well.
5. Line a 9 x 9 inch (22 x 22 cm) pan with greased wax paper and spread the batter.
6. Bake for 45 to 50 minutes.

# Date Oatmeal Cake

| | | |
|---|---|---|
| 1/2 cup | flour | 125 mL |
| 1 tsp | baking soda | 5 mL |
| 1 tsp | cinnamon | 5 mL |
| 1 tsp | cloves | 5 mL |
| 2 cups | rolled oats | 500 mL |
| 3/4 cup | butter | 175 mL |
| 2 cups | brown sugar | 500 mL |
| 2 | eggs | 2 |
| 1 1/2 cups | finely chopped dates | 375 mL |
| 1 cup | coarsely chopped walnuts | 250 mL |

TOPPING

| | | |
|---|---|---|
| 5 tbsp | brown sugar | 75 mL |
| 3 tbsp | butter | 45 mL |
| 3 tbsp | cream | 45 mL |
| 3/4 cup | shredded coconut | 175 mL |

1. Preheat oven to 350°F (180°C). Grease an 8 inch square pan.

2. Sift flour, soda and spices into a bowl.

3. Pour 1 cup (250 mL) of boiling water over the rolled oats and mix well. Cool for a few minutes.

4. Blend the butter, brown sugar, eggs, dates and walnuts into the oatmeal mixture.

5. Pour the oatmeal mixture into the dry ingredients and mix well.

6. Pour into the cake pan and bake for about 45 minutes.

**TOPPING**

7. Combine brown sugar, butter and cream. Boil for 3 minutes.

8. Add coconut and mix. Spread over the cake.

9. Return cake to the oven and brown lightly.

# Christmas Baking

Every December the university community looks forward to the UBC Bakeshop's special Christmas baking. The treats are sold individually and in an assortment of gift packages.

Included here are some of our favourite recipes collected from near and far. However, you don't have to wait for Christmas to enjoy these treats.

# English Christmas Pudding

| | | |
|---|---|---|
| 1/4 lb | margarine | 125 g |
| 1/2 cup | brown sugar | 125 mL |
| 2 | eggs | 2 |
| 2/3 cup | raisins | 150 mL |
| 2/3 cup | sultanas | 150 mL |
| 1/3 cup | currants | 75 mL |
| 1/6 cup | glazed cherries | 38 mL |
| 1/3 cup | dates | 75 mL |
| 1/3 cup | figs | 75 mL |
| 1/3 cup | blanched almonds | 75 mL |
| 1/2 cup | grated apple | 125 mL |
| 1/2 cup | grated carrot | 125 mL |
| 1/2 | lemon, juice and rind | 1/2 |
| 1 tbsp | brandy | 15 mL |
| 1 tbsp | sherry | 15 mL |
| 1/4 cup | white bread crumbs | 50 mL |
| 1/2 cup | all-purpose flour | 125 mL |
| 1/2 tsp | mixed spice | 2 mL |
| 1/4 tsp | nutmeg | 1 mL |
| 1/4 tsp | cinnamon | 1 mL |
| 1/4 tsp | baking soda | 1 mL |
| 1/2 cup | plum jam | 125 mL |

1. Chop fruit and nuts, add apple, carrot and lemon.

2. Pour brandy and sherry over mixture and let stand overnight.

3. Cream margarine and sugar; add eggs. Beat well.

4. Add bread crumbs and jam.

5. Combine flour, mixed spice, nutmeg, cinnamon and soda.

6. Fold in fruit, alternately with dry ingredients. Mix well.

7. Pour into greased Pyrex bowl. Cover and steam for 3 hours. Serve with hard sauce.

# Boiled Dark Fruitcake

*If you like dark, moist, spicy fruitcakes, this one is for you! The method is unusual, but easy. It may be iced or served plain. Delicious also with port wine and aged cheddar.*

| | | |
|---|---|---|
| 1 lb | raisins | 500 g |
| 1 lb | currants | 500 g |
| 1/2 lb | dates | 250 g |
| 1/2 lb | cherries | 250 g |
| 1/2 cup | walnuts | 125 mL |
| 1/2 cup | mixed fruit | 125 mL |
| 2 cups | water | 500 mL |
| 2 cups | brown sugar | 500 mL |
| 1 cup | butter | 250 mL |
| 1 tsp | cinnamon | 5 mL |
| 1 tsp | cloves | 5 mL |
| 1 tsp | allspice | 5 mL |
| 1 tsp | vanilla | 5 mL |
| 3 cups | flour | 750 mL |
| 2 ~~tbsp~~ tsp. | baking soda | 10 mL |

1. Preheat oven to 300°F (150°C).
2. Prepare and cut up fruit. Add all remaining ingredients and place in a large pot.
3. Simmer on top of stove for 15 minutes.
4. Let cool a little, then add flour and baking soda and mix well.
5. Bake 2 1/2 to 3 hours.

# Chef Erich's Brandy Sauce

*This much sought after recipe is from the past UBC Faculty Club. It was enjoyed every year at the Faculty Club Christmas Luncheon Buffets and catered events. Guests came to the club just to have a little pudding with this wonderful sauce.*

| | | |
|---|---|---|
| **1 cup** | **heavy cream** | **250 mL** |
| **1 cup** | **sugar** | **250 mL** |
| **2** | **juice of 2 lemons and 2 oranges** | **2** |
| **4 tsp** | **finely grated lemon peel** | **20 mL** |
| **12** | **egg yolks** | **12** |
| **1 1/3 cup** | **butter (melted)** | **325 mL** |
| **3/4 cup** | **brandy** | **175 mL** |

1. Pour cream into small bowl.
2. Sit bowl in ice bath and beat the cream until thick and glossy, but not stiff. Refrigerate.
3. Beat egg yolks until thick and lemon-coloured, gradually adding the sugar.
4. Slowly beat in the butter, lemon juice, orange juice and brandy.
5. Fold in the lemon peel and whipped cream.
6. Chill thoroughly.

# UBC Hard Sauce

*This is a traditional sauce to serve with Christmas pudding.*

| | | |
|---|---|---|
| 3 – 4 cups | icing sugar | 750 mL – 1 L |
| 1 cup | butter | 250 mL |
| 3 tbsp | rum or brandy | 45 mL |

1. Beat the butter until soft.
2. Gradually add the icing sugar and rum to the butter and beat. Add as much sugar as can be absorbed by the butter. The mixture should be firm and light coloured.
3. Spoon into a fancy dish and swirl with a knife. If desired, decorate with maraschino cherries.
4. Chill thoroughly until ready to serve.

# Vanilla Custard Sauce

*Another delicious sauce to serve with Christmas pudding.*

| | | |
|---|---|---|
| 2 cups | milk | 500 mL |
| 4 | slightly beaten egg yolks | 4 |
| 3 tbsp | sugar | 45 mL |
| 2 tbsp | flour | 30 mL |
| | dash of salt | |
| 2 tsp | vanilla | 10 mL |

1. Scald the milk in a pot.
2. Mix the rest of the ingredients together in the top of a double boiler.
3. Slowly whisk the scalded milk into the other ingredients.
4. Cook while stirring constantly until the mixture thickens.
5. Stir in the vanilla. Strain the custard through a sieve.
6. Serve warm on mince tarts, cake or Christmas pudding. Refrigerate if not used immediately.

# Almond Crescents

*Sophisticated, nutty and delicious.*

| | | |
|---|---|---|
| 1/2 cup | icing sugar, sifted | 125 mL |
| 1 cup | butter | 250 mL |
| 2 cups | all-purpose flour | 500 mL |
| 1/2 tsp | salt | 2 mL |
| 1 cup | slivered almonds, toasted | 250 mL |
| 1 tsp | vanilla or almond extract | 5 mL |

1. Preheat oven to 350°F (180°C).
2. Cream icing sugar and butter.
3. Add vanilla or almond extract and slivered almonds.
4. Add salt to flour and knead into the butter mixture by hand until completely mixed.
5. Chill dough and roll it to the thickness of 1/4 inch (.5 cm). Cut or form into crescent shapes.
6. Bake on greased cookie sheet for 15 minutes. When baked, dip them in icing sugar, if desired.

# Christmas Cake Cookies

*These festive cookies are interesting in their use of Christmas fruits and nuts. They are ideal for Christmas giving and entertaining.*

| | | |
|---|---|---|
| 1 cup | butter | 250 mL |
| 1 1/2 cups | brown sugar | 375 mL |
| 3 | eggs | 3 |
| 2 1/2 cups | all-purpose flour | 625 mL |
| 1 tsp | baking soda | 5 mL |
| 1 tsp | salt | 5 mL |
| 1 tsp | cinnamon | 5 mL |
| 2 lbs | chopped dates | 900 g |
| 1/2 lb | chopped red cherries | 225 g |
| 1/2 lb | chopped candied pineapple | 225 g |
| 1/2 lb | chopped Brazil nuts | 225 g |
| 1/2 lb | toasted slivered almonds | 225 g |

1. Preheat oven to 350°F (180°C). Grease cookie sheet.
2. Cream butter and brown sugar. Add eggs and beat until blended.
3. Mix flour, baking soda, salt and cinnamon in a bowl. Slowly add to the butter, sugar and egg mixture, stirring to mix.
4. Add the fruit and nuts and stir.
5. Drop by teaspoons onto cookie sheet.
6. Bake 10 to 12 minutes.

# English Toffee

*Absolutely delicious, but you must be prepared to stand at the stove for what may seem like hours while the candy thermometer rises to 280°F. Watch out Laura Secord!*

| | | |
|---|---|---|
| 1/2 lb | walnuts or almonds, ground | 230 g |
| 1 lb | milk chocolate, grated | 500 g |
| 2 1/2 cups | sugar | 625 mL |
| 2 cups | butter | 500 mL |
| 4 tbsp | light corn syrup | 60 mL |
| 1/3 lb | walnuts or almonds, finely chopped | 140 g |
| 1 cup | water | 250 mL |

1. Spread half of the ground nuts in a thin, even layer over the bottom of an ungreased baking sheet or two 9 inch (22 cm) cake pans. Then spread half of the chocolate in an even layer over the nuts.

2. Combine the sugar, butter, corn syrup, chopped nuts, and water in a heavy saucepan and place over medium heat.

3. Cook, stirring constantly with a heavy wooden spoon, until a candy thermometer reads 280°F (140°C).

4. Immediately pour the syrup over the nut and chocolate layers. Let cool for 10 minutes.

5. Sprinkle the remaining grated chocolate evenly over the cooling syrup; then sprinkle on the remaining ground nuts.

6. Let stand for at least 5 hours – then break into bite-size pieces. Store in tightly covered containers.

**Suggestion:**
Pack the toffee in doily-lined glass jars and tie a green velvet ribbon around the collars of the jars, or pack in decorative tins.

# Christmas Cherry Bars

*Christmas flavours and colours to get you into the spirit of the season.*

---

| | | |
|---|---|---|
| **CRUST & FILLING** | | |
| 1 cup | all-purpose flour | 250 mL |
| 1 cup | rolled oats | 250 mL |
| 1 cup | packed brown sugar | 250 mL |
| 1 tsp | baking soda | 5 mL |
| 1/4 tsp | salt | 1 mL |
| 1/2 cup | butter | 125 mL |
| 2 | eggs | 2 |
| 1 cup | packed brown sugar | 250 mL |
| 1/4 tsp | almond extract | 1 mL |
| 2 tbsp | flour | 30 mL |
| 1 tsp | baking powder | 5 mL |
| 1/2 tsp | salt | 2 mL |
| 1 cup | coconut | 250 mL |
| 1 cup | halved maraschino cherries | 250 mL |
| 1/2 cup | pecan halves | 125 mL |
| **ICING** | | |
| 1/4 cup | butter | 50 mL |
| 1/2 tsp | almond extract | 2 mL |
| 2 cups | sifted icing sugar | 500 mL |
| 3 – 4 tbsp | milk or cream | 45 – 60 mL |

---

1. Preheat oven to 350°F (180°C). Grease 13 x 9 x 2 inch (32 x 22 x 5 cm) pan.

2. Mix flour, rolled oats, 1 cup (250 mL) brown sugar, soda and 1/4 tsp (1 mL) salt. Add butter and mix until crumbly.

*continued on next page...*

*continued...*

# Christmas Cherry Bars

3. Press into pan and bake 10 minutes.

4. Beat eggs. Stir in 1 cup (250 mL) brown sugar and almond extract.

5. Mix flour, baking powder and ½ tsp (2 mL) salt and stir into egg mixture. Add coconut and cherries. Spread evenly over crust. Sprinkle with pecans.

6. Bake 25 minutes or until lightly browned. Cool completely.

**ICING**

7. Beat all ingredients together until smooth and creamy. Spread over bars.

# Dutch Squares

*A Christmas tradition in the home of one of our retired UBC Food Group managers. This Christmas treat will make you think you were in Amsterdam – if only for a moment.*

| | | |
|---|---|---|
| 3/4 cup | butter | 175 mL |
| 1 cup | brown sugar, packed | 250 mL |
| 3 tbsp | milk | 45 mL |
| 2 3/4 cups | sifted all purpose flour | 675 mL |
| 1 tbsp | cinnamon | 15 mL |
| 1/2 tsp | mace | 2 mL |
| 1/2 tsp | ground aniseed | 2 mL |
| 1/4 tsp | ginger | 1 mL |
| 1/4 tsp | nutmeg | 1 mL |
| 1/4 tsp | cloves | 1 mL |
| 1/4 tsp | baking powder | 1 mL |
| 1/8 tsp | salt | .5 mL |
| 2 cups | blanched almonds, finely ground | 500 mL |
| 3 cups | sifted icing sugar | 750 mL |
| 2 | eggs lightly beaten | 2 |
| 2 tbsp | lemon juice | 30 mL |
| 1 1/2 tsp | almond extract | 7 mL |
| 60 | whole blanched almonds | 60 |

1. Preheat oven to 375°F (190°C). Grease a 15 x 10 x 1 inch (37 x 25 x 2.5 cm) jelly roll pan thoroughly.

2. Cream butter and brown sugar together until fluffy. Beat in milk.

3. Sift flour, spices, baking powder and salt together and add to creamed mixture 1/2 cup at a time, beating well after first few additions and then blending well as dough gets stiffer.

4. Gather the dough into a ball and chill a few minutes so that it is easy to handle.

*continued on next page...*

*continued...*

# Dutch Squares

5. Combine ground almonds and icing sugar while dough is chilling.

6. Add eggs, lemon juice and almond extract, blending in very well. Set aside.

7. Divide dough into two (2) equal parts. Shape one part into a slightly flattened rectangle with your hands and put it on a long piece of waxed paper. Cover with another piece of waxed paper and roll the dough into a rectangle about 15½ inches long and 10½ inches wide (38 cm long and 26 cm wide). Dampen table top before rolling so wax paper will stay in place.

8. Strip waxed paper off dough and invert the dough on the bottom waxed paper into the prepared pan. Strip off waxed paper and press the dough with fingers into the corners and slightly up sides of the pan.

9. Drop the almond mixture by small spoonfuls all over top of dough and spread or pat it gently and evenly almost to the edge of the dough.

10. Roll other half of dough in the same way as the first (use new sheets of waxed paper so dough doesn't stick and trim off any rough edges).

11. Invert it over the almond mixture. Patch the corners with trimmings if necessary. With the edge of a rubber scraper, push the top dough down along the sides of the pan to seal the almond mixture inside.

12. Mark the top of the dough into squares with the tines of a fork, making 6 lines of fork holes lengthwise and 10 crosswise. Centre each square with a whole almond.

13. Bake 20 minutes or until nicely browned.

14. Cool for a few minutes in the pan then turn out onto a large cooling rack to finish cooling. Cut or break into squares and serve. Makes 60 squares.

# Danish Almond Shortbread

*An exciting shortbread recipe that will surprise your guests.*

| | | |
|---|---|---|
| 1 lb | unsalted butter | 450 g |
| 1 3/4 cups | fine granulated sugar | 450 mL |
| 2 | eggs, beaten | 2 |
| 4 1/2 cups | all-purpose flour | 1.125 L |
| 1/4 tsp | baking soda | 1 mL |
| 1/2 tsp | salt | 2 mL |
| 1 cup | finely chopped almonds | 250 mL |
| 1 tsp | almond extract | 5 mL |
| 3/4 cup | broken pieces of almond paste | 175 mL |

1. Have the butter at room temperature before creaming it with the sugar to the consistency of whipped cream.

2. Add eggs and beat again a few minutes.

3. Sift flour with baking soda and salt, gradually add to creamed mixture, then mix until smooth.

4. Add chopped almonds, extract and paste pieces, blending well.

5. Line a 15 x 10 inch (37 x 25 cm) pan lined with wax paper. Pat mixture into pan, cover with waxed paper and chill over night.

6. The next day invert contents onto a board and cut dough into strips 2 1/2 x 1/2 inch (6 x 1 cm).

7. Place on an ungreased baking sheet and bake in oven 325°F (160° C) 20 – 30 minutes or until golden brown.

8. Remove from sheet and let cool on wire racks.

Makes 116 – 120.

# Rolled Oats Shortbread

*Add rolled oats to get an interesting variation on shortbread.*

| | | |
|---|---|---|
| 1 3/4 cup | all purpose flour | 425 mL |
| 1 tsp | baking powder | 5 mL |
| 1/4 tsp | salt | 1 mL |
| 1 cup | soft butter | 250 mL |
| 1/2 cup | brown sugar | 125 mL |
| 1/4 cup | granulated sugar | 50 mL |
| 1/2 tsp | vanilla extract | 125 mL |
| 1 1/2 cups | rolled oats | 375 mL |

**1.** Preheat oven to 325°F (190°C) and grease a baking sheet.

**2.** Sift the flour with the baking powder and salt.

**3.** Cream the margarine, then with your hand gradually add sugars, vanilla extract and rolled oats.

**4.** Still using your hands, gradually add enough of the sifted dry mixture to make a stiff dough.

**5.** Turn on to a floured board and knead dough lightly to blend thoroughly.

**6.** Pat or roll into a 9 x 12 inch (22 x 30 cm) rectangle and cut into 1 1/2 inch (3 cm) squares.

**7.** Bake 20 – 30 minutes or until golden brown.

**8.** Remove from the sheet and let cool on a wire rack.

Makes 45 – 50 cookies.

# Traditional Scottish Shortbread

*Make lots extra for Hogmanay.*

| | | |
|---|---|---|
| 1/2 cup | berry sugar | 125 mL |
| 1 1/2 cups | all-purpose flour | 375 mL |
| 1 cup | butter | 250 mL |
| 1/2 cup | cornstarch | 125 mL |

1. Preheat oven to 300°F (150°C).
2. Cream butter and sugar. Fold in flour and cornstarch.
3. Press into greased 8 x 8 inch (20 cm) pan. Score top.
4. Bake for 1 1/4 – 1 1/2 hours.
5. Sprinkle with berry sugar. Cut while hot into bars.

# Brown Sugar Shortbread

*Simple but delicious. The dough may be rolled, cut into shapes and decorated.*

| | | |
|---|---|---|
| 1 cup | butter | 250 mL |
| 2 1/4 cup | flour | 550 mL |
| 3/4 cup | brown sugar | 175 mL |

1. Preheat oven to 325°F (160°C).
2. Mix all ingredients together.
3. Roll and cut into shapes.
4. Bake for 10 minutes.

# UBC Whipped Shortbread

*See how easy it is to bake one of our favourite Christmas treats.*

| | | |
|---|---|---|
| **1 cup** | **butter** | **50 mL** |
| **1/2 cup** | **icing sugar** | **125 mL** |
| **2 cups** | **sifted all-purpose flour** | **500 mL** |
| **1/2 tsp** | **salt** | **2 mL** |
| **1/2 tsp** | **vanilla** | **2 mL** |

**1.** Preheat oven to 350°F (180°C).

**2.** Cream butter and sugar. Add remaining ingredients and whip until light and fluffy.

**3.** Pipe into desired shape onto a cookie sheet.

**4.** Bake for 20 minutes or until lightly golden.

Makes 5 dozen.

# Christmas Stollen

*This recipe was published in the UBC Bookstore Newsletter many years ago. Stollen is a German tradition, but is now enjoyed all over Canada. Excellent with butter at breakfast time or as an alternative to Christmas Cake.*

| | | |
|---|---|---|
| **6 3/4 cups** | **flour** | **1.7 L** |
| **2 tbsp** | **baking powder** | **30 mL** |
| **1 1/2 cups** | **sugar** | **375 mL** |
| **1/4 tsp** | **cardamom** | **1 mL** |
| **1/4 tsp** | **nutmeg** | **1 mL** |
| **8 drops** | **lemon oil** | **8** |
| **2 tsp** | **vanilla** | **10 mL** |
| **2 tbsp** | **rum** | **30 mL** |
| **4** | **eggs** | **4** |
| **1 1/3 cup** | **butter ( 1/2 lb)** | **325 mL** |
| **1/2 cup** | **lard** | **125 mL** |
| **1 pkg** | **baking cottage cheese** | **250 g** |
| **1/2 cup** | **mixed peel** | **125 mL** |
| **1 1/3 cup** | **raisins** | **325 mL** |
| **1 1/3 cups** | **currants** | **325 mL** |
| **1 cup** | **flaked almonds** | **250 mL** |
| **1/4 cup** | **citron** | **50 mL** |

**1.** Preheat oven to 350°F (180°C).

**2.** Sift together flour and baking powder.

**3.** In a separate bowl mix together sugar, cardamom, nutmeg, lemon oil, vanilla, rum and 4 eggs. Add to the flour mixture.

**4.** Cut butter and lard into cubes and work it into the flour mixture.

*continued on next page...*

*continued...*

## Christmas Stollen

5. Add cottage cheese, mixed peel, raisins, currants, almonds and citron.

6. Mix well with hands, until dough is smooth (some lard and butter pieces will show).

7. Divide dough into three pieces. Turn each piece onto a lightly floured board and roll into an oblong shape about ½" (1 cm) thick. Fold one side of the dough lengthwise over the other side so that the upper half covers ¾ of the lower half. Shape the loaves high as they will flatten out in the oven.

8. Bake for about one hour on a cookie sheet lined with two layers of brown paper (i.e. paper grocery bags) cut to fit a large cookie sheet).

9. Remove from oven. Drizzle with melted butter and dust with icing sugar while still warm.

# Cookies

Cookies are the *daily treat.* Unlike other pastries such as pie or cake, usually we can have one or two cookies without worrying about those extra calories. Cookies are the perfect accompaniment for ice cold milk, steaming hot tea or coffee.

# Sugar Cookies

*A classic standard which can inspire the baker to special event fantasies. Cut in shapes for special occasions: trees, stars and Santas for Christmas; pumpkins and witches for Halloween; shamrocks for St Patrick's Day – the opportunities are endless.*

| | | |
|---|---|---|
| 2 1/2 cups | all-purpose flour | 625 mL |
| 1 tsp | baking soda | 5 mL |
| 1 tsp | cream of tartar | 5 mL |
| 1/4 tsp | salt | 1 mL |
| 1 cup | softened butter | 250 mL |
| 1 3/4 cup | icing sugar | 425 mL |
| 1 | large egg | 1 |
| 1 tsp | vanilla | 5 mL |

1. Preheat oven to 400°F (200°C).
2. Stir together dry ingredients (except sugar).
3. Cream butter and gradually beat in sugar; beat in egg and vanilla.
4. Blend in dry ingredients a little at a time. If necessary, chill dough.
5. Roll out dough into 1/4 inch (5mm) thickness. Cut into desired shapes. Place on ungreased baking sheet.
6. Bake for 7 to 8 minutes. Makes 2 dozen large cookies.

# UBC Gourmet Cookies

*The chocolate lovers cookie which is a standard on UBC Coffee Shop and Cafeteria counters.*

| | | |
|---|---|---|
| 1/2 cup | unsalted butter, room temp | 125 g |
| 3/4 cup | packed dark brown sugar | 175 mL |
| 1/4 cup | sugar | 50 mL |
| 1 tsp | vanilla | 5 mL |
| 1/4 tsp | salt | 2 mL |
| 1/3 cup | chunky-style peanut butter | 75 mL |
| 1 | egg | 1 |
| 1/2 tsp | baking soda | 2 mL |
| 1 cup | all-purpose flour | 250 mL |
| 3/4 cup | coarsely chopped unsalted roasted peanuts | 175 mL |
| 2 cups | coarsely chopped semisweet chocolate | 375 mL |

1. Preheat oven to 350°F (180°C). Grease baking sheets.
2. In a large mixing bowl, combine butter, brown sugar, sugar, vanilla and salt. Beat with a spoon until fluffy.
3. Beat in the peanut butter, egg and baking soda.
4. Stir in the flour and then the peanuts and chocolate.
5. Transfer to a bowl just large enough for the dough, cover and refrigerate until firm, about four hours or overnight.
6. Using 2 to 3 tbsp of dough for each cookie, shape into balls and place in centre of cookie sheet. Evenly space four others a few inches from each corner.
7. Bake for 10 to 12 minutes, or until the cookie springs back when lightly touched. Overbaking will result in dry cookies.
8. Cool on the sheets for 2 minutes and transfer to a rack to cool. Makes 20 to 32 cookies *(UBC size!)*

# Biscotti

These nut studded, twice-baked, Italian cookies have become incredibly popular in recent years. Tuscans serve them after dinner to dip in their rich sweet wine. Vancouverites enjoy them dipped in gourmet coffees.

# Almond Apricot Biscotti

*This is one of our favourite recipes and sure to win you rave reviews.*

| | | |
|---|---|---|
| **2 3/4 cups** | **sifted-all purpose flour** | **675 mL** |
| **1 1/2 cups** | **sugar** | **375 mL** |
| **1/2 cup** | **chilled unsalted butter** | **125 mL** |
| **2 1/2 tsp** | **baking powder** | **12 mL** |
| **1 tsp** | **salt** | **5 mL** |
| **1 tsp** | **ground ginger** | **5 mL** |
| **3 1/2 oz.** | **imported white chocolate, finely chopped** | **100 g** |
| **1 2/3 cups** | **whole almonds, toasted, coarsely chopped** | **400 mL** |
| **2** | **large eggs** | **2** |
| **1/4 cup + 1 tbsp** | **apricot flavoured brandy** | **65 mL** |
| **2 tsp** | **almond extract** | **10 mL** |
| **1– 6 oz. pkg** | **dried apricots, diced** | **170 g** |

1. Preheat oven to 350°F (180°C).

2. Line a 18 x 12 x 1 inch (45 x 30 X 2.5 cm) cookie sheet with foil. Butter and flour foil.

3. Sift together flour, baking powder and salt. Add sugar and ground ginger, stirring well.

*continued...*

## Almond Apricot Biscotti

4. Cut butter into the flour mixture with a pastry blender until fine meal forms. Stir in white chocolate and almonds.

5. Beat eggs, brandy and extract to blend in a large bowl. Add flour mixture and apricots and stir until moist dough forms.

6. Drop dough by spoonfuls onto the cookie sheet. Using moistened fingertips, shape the dough into three 12 inch (30 cm) long strips, spacing evenly. The strips should be 2 inches (4 cm) wide.

7. Refrigerate until dough is firm, about 30 minutes.

8. Position rack in centre of preheated oven. Bake until logs are golden, about 30 minutes.

9. Transfer to rack and cool completely.

10. Reduce heat to 300°F (150°C). Cut logs from sides of pan if necessary. Transfer to work surface.

11. Using heavy sharp knife, firmly cut each log crosswise into 3/4 inch wide slices (2 cm).

12. Arrange half the cookies cut-side down on cookie sheet.

13. Bake 10 minutes. Gently turn cookies over and bake 10 minutes longer.

14. Transfer cookies to racks. Repeat baking with remaining cookies. Cool cookies completely.

(Can be prepared 2 weeks ahead. Store in airtight container at room temperature).

# Anise Biscotti

*A traditional biscotti recipe with anise and almonds.*

| | | |
|---|---|---|
| 1 1/4 cups | toasted almonds (5 oz.) | 300 mL |
| 1/2 cup | butter, room temperature | 125 mL |
| 1 cup | sugar | 250 mL |
| 2 | eggs | 2 |
| 1 tbsp | anisette liqueur | 15 mL |
| 1 1/2 tsp | baking powder | 7 mL |
| 1/4 tsp | salt | 1 mL |
| 2 1/4 cup | all-purpose flour | 50 mL |
| 1/2 cup | coarse yellow cornmeal | 125 mL |
| 1 1/2 tbsp | aniseed | 25 mL |

1. Preheat oven to 325°F (160°C). Butter 2 cookie sheets.
2. Coarsely chop 1/4 cup (50 mL) almonds.
3. Cream butter with sugar in large bowl just until combined.
4. Beat in eggs, liqueur, baking powder and salt.
5. Stir in 2 cups (500 mL) flour, cornmeal, then whole and chopped almonds and aniseed. If dough is sticky, mix in enough of remaining 1/4 cup (50 mL) flour by the tablespoon (15 mL) to form smooth dough.
6. Shape dough into four 2 inch (5 cm) wide x 3/4 inch (2 cm) high logs. Transfer to cookie sheets, spacing evenly.
7. Bake until pale golden on edges – about 35 minutes.

*continued...*

## Anise Biscotti

8. Transfer logs to racks and cool for 10 minutes. Maintain oven temperature.
9. Place logs on work surface and cut diagonally into ½ inch (1.5 cm) thick slices.
10. Arrange slices cut side down on cookie sheets.
11. Bake until light golden – about 10 minutes. Gently turn cookies over and bake 10 minutes longer.
12. Transfer biscotti to rack and cool completely. Store in airtight container at room temperature.

Makes approximately 4 ½ dozen.

# Orange and Cinnamon Biscotti

| | | |
|---|---|---|
| 1/2 cup | butter, room temperature | 125 mL |
| 1 cup | sugar | 250 mL |
| 2 | eggs | 2 |
| 2 tsp | grated orange peel | 10 mL |
| 1 tsp | vanilla extract | 5 mL |
| 1 1/2 tsp | baking powder | 7 mL |
| 2 cups | all-purpose flour | 500 mL |
| 1 tsp | ground cinnamon | 5 mL |
| 1/4 tsp | salt | 1 mL |

1. Preheat oven to 325°F (160°C). Butter 2 cookie sheets.
2. Cream butter with sugar in large bowl just until combined.
3. Beat in eggs, orange rind and vanilla.
4. Stir flour, baking powder, cinnamon and salt in a bowl.
5. Add dry ingredients to the butter mixture and combine.
6. Divide dough in half. With lightly floured hands, form each half into a 3 inch (7.5 cm) wide x 3/4 inch (2 cm) high log. Transfer to cookie sheets, spacing evenly.
7. Bake until pale golden on edges – about 35 minutes.
8. Transfer logs to racks and cool for 10 minutes. Maintain oven temperature.

*continued...*

# Orange and Cinnamon Biscotti

9. Place logs on work surface and cut diagonally into ½ inch (1.25 cm) thick slices.

10. Arrange slices cut side down on cookie sheets.

11. Bake until the bottom side is light golden – about 12 minutes.

12. Turn the biscotti over and bake for about another 12 minutes or until both sides are golden.

13. Transfer biscotti to rack and cool completely. Store in airtight container at room temperature.

# Gingersnaps

*An old fashioned dipping cookie and a change from biscotti.*

| | | |
|---|---|---|
| 1/2 cup | shortening | 125 mL |
| 1 cup | sugar | 250 mL |
| 1/4 cup | molasses | 50 mL |
| 1 | large egg | 1 |
| 2 cups | all purpose flour | 500 mL |
| 2 tsp | baking soda | 10 mL |
| 1/2 tsp | salt | 2 mL |
| 1 tbsp | ground ginger | 15 mL |
| 1 tsp | ground cinnamon | 5 mL |
| 1/4 tsp | ground cloves | 1 mL |
| | sugar for rolling | |

1. Preheat oven to 350°F (180°C). Grease a baking sheet.

2. Cream together the shortening and 1 cup of sugar.

3. Stir in the molasses and then the egg.

4. Combine the dry ingredients and blend into the creamed mixture.

5. Form the dough into one inch balls and roll in the sugar.

6. Place on the baking sheet about two inches apart and bake about 15 minutes. As the balls melt down, the cookies develop their characteristic texture.

Makes about 3 dozen cookies.

# Desserts

A fitting end to a good meal is a sweet, satisfying, artistically served dessert. In addition to our regular pastries, the UBC Bakeshop also makes a wide variety of desserts for the cafeterias and special catered events.

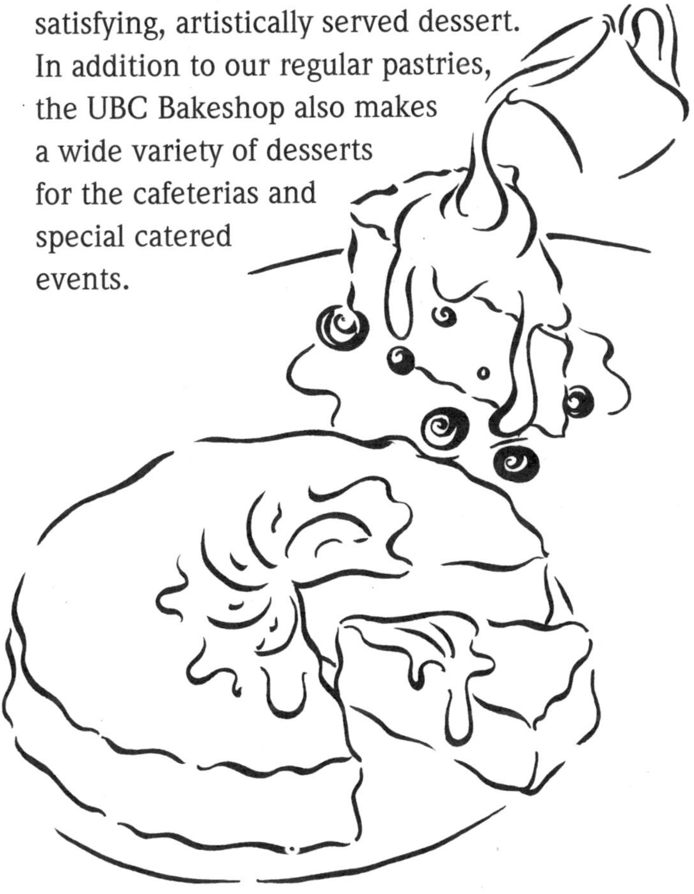

# Apple Betty

*An old fashioned dessert similar to Apple Crisp. It's universally enjoyed, especially when served warm with ice cream.*

| | | |
|---|---|---|
| **6 to 7** | **apples, peeled and sliced** | **6 to 7** |
| | **cinnamon to taste** | |

**TOPPING**

| | | |
|---|---|---|
| **1/2 cup** | **butter** | **125 mL** |
| **1 cup** | **brown sugar** | **250 mL** |
| **1 cup** | **flour** | **250 mL** |
| **1/4 tsp** | **salt** | **1 mL** |
| **1/2 tsp** | **cinnamon** | **2 mL** |

**1.** Preheat oven to 350°F (180°C).

**2.** Fill small 1.5 quart (1.5 L) casserole dish 2/3 full with sliced apples. If the apples are tart, you may want to add 1/4 cup (50 mL) white sugar.

**TOPPING**

**3.** Cream butter and brown sugar.

**4.** Add flour, salt and cinnamon and rub to a crumbly mixture. Sprinkle over apples.

**5.** Bake for 40 minutes.

Serves 6.

# Fruit Cocktail Dessert Cake

*Keep a can of fruit cocktail on hand to make this quick delicious dessert. Serve it cool, or warm with whipped cream or ice cream.*

| | | |
|---|---|---|
| 1 1/2 cups | sugar | 375 mL |
| 2 cups | flour | 500 mL |
| 2 tsp | baking soda | 10 mL |
| 1/2 tsp | salt | 2 mL |
| 2 | eggs | 2 |
| 14 oz. can | fruit cocktail, with juice | 430 mL |
| **ICING** | | |
| 3/4 cup | sugar | 175 mL |
| 1/2 cup | light cream or milk | 125 mL |
| 1/2 cup | butter | 125 mL |
| 1 tsp | vanilla or brandy | 5 mL |

**1.** Preheat oven to 350°F (180°C).

**2.** Beat eggs slightly.

**3.** Add all ingredients except flour.

**4.** Add flour last.

**5.** Bake in 9 x 13 inch (22 x 33 cm) pan for 45 minutes.

**ICING**

**6.** Boil all ingredients except vanilla.

**7.** Remove from heat.

**8.** Add vanilla, pour over the hot cake – it makes a lot but use all of it.

**9.** Serve warm with whipped cream or vanilla ice-cream. It keeps refrigerated for several days.

# Blueberry Apple Crisp

*Another old fashioned dessert which like Apple Betty is best served warm with cream or ice cream.*

| | | |
|---|---|---|
| **4 cups** | **peeled, cored and sliced apples** | **1 L** |
| **1 cup** | **fresh or frozen blueberries** | **250 mL** |
| **1/4 cup** | **sugar** | **50 mL** |
| **1/2 cup** | **all-purpose flour** | **125 mL** |
| **1 cup** | **brown sugar** | **250 mL** |
| **1 cup** | **quick-cooking oats** | **250 mL** |
| **1 tsp** | **baking powder** | **5 mL** |
| **1 tsp** | **ground cinnamon** | **5 mL** |
| **1/4 tsp** | **salt** | **1 mL** |
| **1/2 cup** | **butter at room temperature** | **125 mL** |

**1.** Preheat oven to 350°F (180°C).

**2.** Combine apples, blueberries and sugar in 2 quart (2 L) casserole.

**3.** Combine flour, brown sugar, oats, baking powder, cinnamon and salt.

**4.** With a fork, blend butter into flour mixture to form coarse crumbs. Sprinkle over fruit.

**5.** Bake for 45 to 60 minutes.

Makes 4 to 6 servings.

# Blueberry and Lemon Mousse

*Light and refreshing – a perfect finishing touch on a hot summer day.*

| | | |
|---|---|---|
| 4 | egg yolks | 4 |
| 1/2 cup | sugar | 125 mL |
| 1/4 cup | lemon juice | 50 mL |
| 2 tsp | grated lemon rind | 10 mL |
| 2 | egg whites | 2 |
| 1/2 cup | heavy cream | 125 mL |
| 1 cup | blueberries | 250 mL |

1. In a bowl, beat the 4 egg yolks until they are thick and pale.
2. Beat in the sugar, lemon juice and grated lemon rind.
3. Cook the mixture in the top of a double boiler over hot water, stirring constantly until it is thick.
4. Let mixture cool.
5. Beat egg whites until stiff.
6. Beat heavy cream until moist peaks form.
7. Fold the egg whites and cream into the lemon mixture and stir in the blueberries.
8. Pour into 4 glasses. Garnish the top with berries and chill.

# Cranberry Cake with Hot Caramel Sauce

*A great winter dessert. Fresh cranberries lend a tart contrast to the sweet caramel sauce.*

| | | |
|---|---|---|
| 2 cups | all-purpose flour | 500 mL |
| 2 cups | sugar | 500 mL |
| 2 tsp | double-acting baking powder | 10 mL |
| 3 tbsp | unsalted butter | 45 mL |
| 1 cup | milk | 250 mL |
| 3 cups | fresh cranberries, picked over and halved | 750 mL |
| 1 tsp | vanilla | 5 mL |

SAUCE

| | | |
|---|---|---|
| 1/2 cup | firmly packed dark brown sugar | 125 mL |
| 1/2 cup | heavy cream | 125 mL |

1. Preheat oven to 350°F (180°C).
2. Into a bowl, sift together the flour, 1 1/2 cups (375 mL) sugar, and baking powder, add 4 tsp (20 mL) of the butter, cut into bits, and combine the mixture until it resembles meal.
3. Stir in milk, vanilla and cranberries.
4. Line the bottom of a buttered 10 inch (25 cm) round baking pan with wax paper and butter and flour the paper.

*continued...*

## Cranberry Cake with Hot Caramel Sauce

5. Pour the batter into the pan and bake the cake in middle of oven for 40 to 45 minutes, or until sides of the cake pull away from the pan slightly.

6. Let cake cool in pan on a rack for 10 minutes and turn it out onto rack. Remove the wax paper and let cake cool completely.

7. In a heavy saucepan combine brown sugar, remaining ½ cup (125 mL) sugar, cream and remaining 5 tsp (25 mL) butter, bringing mixture to a boil over moderately low heat, stirring constantly. Boil, stirring constantly, until sugar is dissolved.

8. Serve sauce with the cake.

# Cinnamon Apple Dumplings

*This dessert was very popular at UBC during the 1980s. It was served with hot custard sauce.*

| | | |
|---|---|---|
| 1 envelope | flaky pie crust mix | 1 |
| 4 | medium apples, peeled and cored | 4 |
| 1/4 cup | sugar | 50 mL |
| 1 tsp | cinnamon | 5 mL |
| 2 tbsp | raisins | 30 mL |
| 1 | egg | 1 |
| 1 tsp | water | 5 mL |
| **SAUCE** | | |
| 1/2 cup | sugar | 125 mL |
| 1 cup | water | 250 mL |
| 2 tbsp | shortening | 30 mL |
| 1/2 tsp | cinnamon | 2 mL |

1. Preheat oven to 400°F (200°C).

2. Prepare pastry according to directions on envelope. Reserve a little for decoration, if desired.

3. Roll out pastry on lightly floured surface to 14 inch (35 cm) square. Cut into four squares. Place an apple in centre of each pastry square.

4. Combine sugar, cinnamon and raisins; spoon into apple cavities.

5. Bring corners of pastry up to centre of apple. Press edges to seal well. Garnish with leaves cut from reserved pastry.

*continued...*

# Cinnamon Apple Dumplings

**6.** Place in 9 inch (22 cm) square baking pan.

**7.** Beat egg and water together; brush over dumplings.

**8.** Bake for 15 minutes.

**9.** While dumplings are baking, prepare the sauce.

**SAUCE**

**10.** Combine all ingredients in small saucepan. Boil for 2 minutes.

**11.** Pour over partially baked dumplings and bake 25 – 30 minutes longer or until crust is deep golden and apples are tender. Baste dumplings often during baking.

**12.** Serve warm with custard sauce. See page 35.

Makes 4 servings.

# Fresh Peach Cobbler

*You may use any fresh fruit with this quick recipe. It's a "golden oldie" enjoyed equally by adults and children.*

| | | |
|---|---|---|
| 3 cups | cut up fresh peaches | 750 mL |
| 2/3 cup | sugar | 150 mL |
| 2 tbsp | flour | 30 mL |
| 1/2 tsp | cinnamon | 2 mL |
| 1 cup | flour | 250 mL |
| 2 tbsp | sugar | 30 mL |
| 1 1/2 tsp | baking powder | 7 mL |
| 1/2 tsp | salt | 2 mL |
| 1/3 cup | oil | 75 mL |
| 3 tbsp | milk | 5 mL |
| 1 | egg | 1 |

1. Preheat oven to 350°F (180°C).
2. Arrange peaches in 8 inch (20 cm) or 9 inch (22 cm) square baking pan.
3. Sprinkle with 2/3 cup (150 mL) sugar, 2 tbsp (30 mL) flour and cinnamon.
4. Sift together flour, sugar, baking powder and salt; add the oil, milk and slightly beaten egg. Stir with fork until blended.
5. Spread over the fruit.
6. Bake for 25 to 30 minutes. Serve with ice cream.

# Grenoble Walnut Tart

*An exotic version of the butter tart. Not for the faint hearted or dieter, but worth every bite... live for today, diet tomorrow.*

**TART SHELL**

| | | |
|---|---|---|
| 1/3 cup | butter/margarine | 5 mL |
| 1/4 cup | sugar | 50 mL |
| 1 | egg yolk | 1 |
| 1 cup | unsifted all-purpose flour | 150 mL |

**FILLING**

| | | |
|---|---|---|
| 2 cups | coarsely chopped walnuts | 500 mL |
| 2/3 cup | light brown sugar, packed | 150 mL |
| 1/4 cup | butter | 50 mL |
| 1/4 cup | dark corn syrup | 50 mL |
| 1/2 cup | heavy cream | 125 mL |

1. Preheat oven to 375°F (190°C).

**TART SHELL**

2. In medium bowl beat 1/3 cup (75 mL) butter with sugar until light and fluffy.

3. Add egg yolk; beat well.

4. Gradually beat in flour until blended (mixture will be crumbly). With hands, form dough into a ball.

5. Press into bottom and sides of a 9 inch (22 cm) fluted tart pan with removable bottom.

6. Bake in centre of oven for 12 minutes or until lightly browned. Cool.

*continued on next page...*

*continued...*

# Grenoble Walnut Tart

**FILLING**

7. Spread nuts on cookie sheet in a single layer.

8. Bake for 5 minutes. Set aside to cool. Sprinkle nuts in bottom of tart shell.

9. In 2-quart (2 L) saucepan stir sugar with butter, syrup and 2 tbsp (30 mL) cream.

10. Over medium heat, bring mixture to a boil, stirring constantly; boil 1 minute. Pour over walnuts.

11. Bake in centre of oven for 10 minutes or until bubbly. Place on rack to cool.

12. Beat remaining cream and serve with tart.

Serves 12.

# Hot Apple Cake with Caramel Sauce

*With apples, walnuts and spices in a classic cream cake, who needs a caramel sauce? But then again why not go ahead and enjoy it.*

CAKE

| | | |
|---|---|---|
| 1 cup | butter | 250 mL |
| 2 | eggs, beaten | 2 |
| 1 tsp | nutmeg | 5 mL |
| 1 tsp | baking soda | 5 mL |
| 3 | apples, peeled and finely chopped | 3 |
| 1 tsp | vanilla | 5 mL |
| 1 cup | sugar | 50 mL |
| 1½ cups | flour | 375 mL |
| 1 tsp | cinnamon | 5 mL |
| ½ tsp | salt | 2 mL |
| ¾ cup | walnuts | 175 mL |

SAUCE

| | | |
|---|---|---|
| 1 cup | sugar | 250 mL |
| 1 cup | whipping cream | 250 mL |
| ⅓ cup | dark rum | 75 mL |
| 1 cup | brown sugar | 250 mL |
| 1 cup | butter | 250 mL |

CAKE

**1.** Preheat oven to 350°F (180°C).

**2.** Cream together butter and sugar. Add eggs.

**3.** Blend together dry ingredients. Add to buttered sugar mixture. Stir in apples, vanilla and nuts. Mix well.

*continued on next page...*

*continued...*

# Hot Apple Cake with Carmel Sauce

**4.** Place in 10 inch (25 cm) deep pie plate.
Bake 3/4 – 1 hour.

**SAUCE**

**5.** Combine sugars and cream in a pan and cook about 1 hour stirring often.

**6.** Add butter and cook 1/2 hour longer.

**7.** Remove from heat and add rum. Serve warm.

**8.** Serve hot with hot sauce or cold with whipped cream or ice cream.

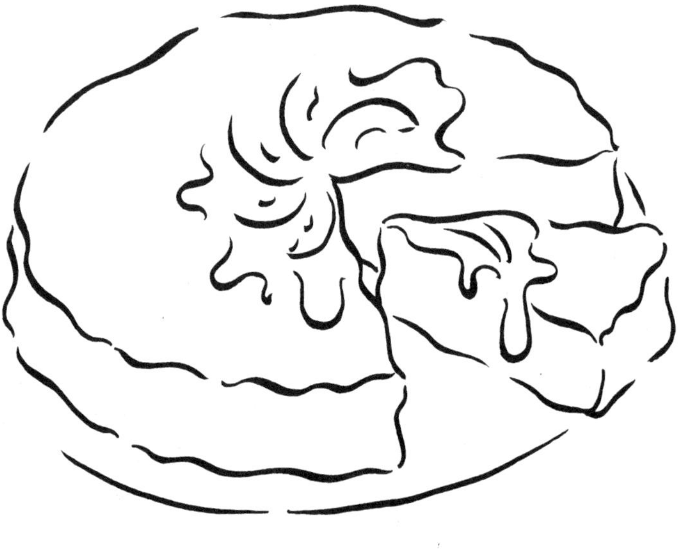

# Old-Fashioned Rice & Raisin Pudding

*This old classic has gained favour in the nineties and should be enjoyed through the next millennium.*

| | | |
|---|---|---|
| 1 3/4 cup | water | 425 mL |
| 1/2 cup | rice | 125 mL |
| 1/2 tsp | salt | 2 mL |
| 2 cups | milk | 500 mL |
| 2 | eggs, beaten | 2 |
| 1/3 cup | sugar | 75 mL |
| 1 tsp | vanilla | 5 mL |
| 1/4 cup | raisins, plumped in water and drained | 50 mL |
| optional | nutmeg or cinnamon | |

1. Preheat oven to 350°F (180°C).
2. Bring water to a boil. Stir in rice and salt.
3. Cover and simmer until all water is absorbed, about 30 minutes.
4. Add milk and boil gently, stirring occasionally, until mixture thickens slightly, about 5 minutes.
5. Combine eggs, sugar and vanilla in a bowl.
6. Gradually stir in rice mixture; mix well.
7. Pour into a greased 1 1/2 quart (1.5 L) casserole.
8. Stir in raisins and sprinkle nutmeg or cinnamon over top.
9. Place casserole in a pan which contains about 1 inch (2 cm) hot water.
10. Bake uncovered for 45 to 50 minutes or until knife inserted near centre comes out clean. Makes 6 servings.

# Peach Bread Pudding

*Bread pudding with added fruit, a custardy texture and crusty top. Comfort food at its best.*

| | | |
|---|---|---|
| 3 | eggs | 3 |
| 1/2 cup | sugar | 125 mL |
| 2 tsp | vanilla | 10 mL |
| pinch | salt | pinch |
| 2 1/2 cups | milk | 625 mL |
| 4 cups | small pieces of slightly dry white bread | 4 |
| 1 cup | sliced peaches | 250 mL |
| 1 tsp | cinnamon | 5 mL |

1. Preheat oven to 350°F (180°C).
2. In bowl, combine eggs, sugar, vanilla and salt; beat until light and fluffy. Add milk; stir to blend well.
3. In greased 8-cup (2 L) baking dish, place bread, then sliced peaches on top of bread.
4. Pour egg mixture on top. Sprinkle with cinnamon.
5. Place dish in shallow pan of hot water.
6. Bake for 45 minutes or until top is slightly crusty and knife inserted in centre comes out clean. Serve warm.

Makes 6 servings.

# Angel's Cloud

*This light and airy dessert is satisfyingly rich and beautiful as a dinner party finale.*

| | | |
|---|---|---|
| 3 | eggs, separated | 3 |
| 1/2 cup | sugar | 125 mL |
| 1 oz. | brandy | 32 mL |
| 1 | envelope gelatin | 1 |
| 1 cup | whipping cream | 250 mL |
| 1 tsp | vanilla | 5 mL |
| 1 oz. | rum | 32 mL |

1. In a large bowl beat egg yolks to light lemon colour, add sugar gradually and continue beating until very stiff. Add rum and brandy.

2. In another bowl beat egg whites until stiff.

3. In another bowl, whip cream until stiff – add vanilla.

4. Soak gelatin in 1/4 cup (50 mL) cold water (leave 5 minutes). Then stir over hot water until dissolved.

5. Stir gelatin into egg yolk mixture, then fold in egg whites and whipped cream.

6. Pour into serving dishes and chill.

7. Decorate with glazed cherries and pecans before serving.

# Pineapple Cheesecake

*This light fluffy dessert is rich and tasty with year-round available crushed pineapple. This is a good recipe to use when fresh fruits are scarce.*

| | | |
|---|---|---|
| 1 – 85 g pkg | lemon Jello | 1 – 85 g pkg |
| 2 cups | boiling water | 500 mL |
| 2 envelopes | unflavoured gelatin | 2 envelopes |
| 1/2 cup | cold water | 125 mL |
| 1 3/4 cups | hot water | 425 mL |
| 2 – 20 oz. cans | crush pineapple, drained | 2/625 mL |
| 8 oz. | cream cheese | 250 mL |
| 1 cup | sour cream | 250 mL |
| 2 cups | whipping cream | 500 mL |
| 1 cup | icing sugar | 250 mL |

1. Dissolve Jello in 2 cups (500 mL) boiling water.
2. Dissolve gelatin in 1/2 cup cold water, add 1 3/4 cups hot water and bring to a boil.
3. Combine Jello and gelatin; cool until partly jelled.
4. In a blender, combine crushed pineapple with 1 1/2 cups (375 mL) of the juice.
5. Combine cheese and sour cream, add to pineapple mixture. Add Jello mixture.
6. Whip cream, adding icing sugar towards the end. Fold into pineapple mixture.
7. Pour into a 3 inch (8 cm) deep crumb lined pan. Refrigerate overnight.
8. Garnish with whipped cream and seasonal fruit. Delicious with chocolate wafer crumbs shell.

# Pineapple Delight

*University students regard anything called "Delight" or "Surprise" with suspicion. Nevertheless, they enjoy Pineapple Delight.*

| | | |
|---|---|---|
| **BOTTOM** | | |
| **2 1/2 cups** | **crushed graham wafers** | **625 mL** |
| **1/2 cup** | **melted butter** | **125 mL** |
| **1st LAYER** | | |
| **1 1/2 cups** | **icing sugar** | **375 mL** |
| **1/2 cup** | **creamed butter** | **125 mL** |
| **2** | **eggs, beaten** | **2** |
| **2nd LAYER** | | |
| **1 cup** | **whipping cream** | **250 mL** |
| **1 – 10 oz.** | **crushed pineapple, drained** | **310 g** |

**1.** Preheat oven to 325°F (160°C).

**BOTTOM**

**2.** Combine graham wafer crumbs and melted butter.

**3.** Mix well and press into bottom of a 9 x 9 inch (22 cm) round pan (reserve a few crumbs to sprinkle on top.

**4.** Bake 10 minutes. Cool.

**1st LAYER**

**5.** Cream until fluffy, icing sugar and butter – add beaten eggs. Mix well.

**2nd LAYER**

**6.** Whip cream; fold in drained, crushed pineapple.

**7.** Spread over 1st layer. Sprinkle a few crumbs over top layer.

**8.** Chill. Cut into squares and serve.

# Rhubarb Crisp

*A seasonal favourite.*

| | | |
|---|---|---|
| 5 cups | sliced rhubarb (1/2 inch or 1 cm slices) | 1.25 L |
| 1 cup | granulated sugar | 250 mL |
| 1 tbsp | flour | 15 mL |
| 1 | large egg, lightly beaten | 1 |
| **TOPPING** | | |
| 1/2 cup | all-purpose flour | 125 mL |
| 1/2 cup | quick-cooking oats | 125 mL |
| 1/3 cup | packed brown sugar | 75 mL |
| 1/4 tsp | ground nutmeg | 1 mL |
| 1/4 cup | butter/margarine | 50 mL |

**1.** Preheat oven to 350°F (180°C).

**2.** Combine rhubarb, granulated sugar, flour and egg in 8 inch (20 cm) round baking dish and mix well.

**TOPPING**

**3.** Combine flour, oats, brown sugar and nutmeg.

**4.** Cut in butter until crumbly. Sprinkle over rhubarb.

**5.** Bake for 45 to 60 minutes or until rhubarb is tender.

Makes 6 servings.

# Crème Caramel

| | | |
|---|---|---|
| **CARAMEL TOPPING** | | |
| 1 cup | sugar | 250 mL |
| 1/2 cup | cold water | 125 mL |
| **CUSTARD** | | |
| 4 cups | milk | 1 L |
| 1 tsp | vanilla extract | 5 mL |
| 2/3 cup | sugar | 225 mL |
| 4 | large eggs | 4 |
| 4 | large egg yolks | 4 |

**CARAMEL TOPPING**

1. Place sugar and water in a small heavy based saucepan. Stir to mix.

2. Place over a low heat and cook, shaking the pan occasionally, until the sugar is dissolved.

3. When dissolved, turn heat to high and boil rapidly. (Do not stir the syrup as it may cause it to crystalize).

4. As the bubbles start to break more slowly than at first, the syrup will gradually start to turn brown.

5. Watch it very carefully and remove from heat as soon as it is a golden brown. If the colour gets too dark the syrup will taste bitter.

6. Pour hot caramel into a six-cup ring mould. Immediately tip mould slightly so the caramel coats the sides. Set aside while preparing the custard.

*continued on next page...*

*continued...*

# Crème Caramel

### CUSTARD

7. Scald milk in medium saucepan by bringing it just to the boil. Remove from the heat and add sugar and vanilla extract. Stir until dissolved.

8. In medium bowl, beat eggs and egg yolks just until blended. Stir in hot milk.

9. Cool slightly and strain into ring mould.

10. Place in a shallow baking or roasting tin with cold water up to ½ inch.

11. Place in centre of 300°F (150°C) oven about 1½ hours. Do not overbake.

12. Crème Caramel is done when it is set and a knife inserted in centre comes out clean. Remove dish from water bath and refrigerate until chilled.

13. To unmould, loosen the edge of the custard with a knife and invert onto a deep serving plate. A certain amount of caramel will remain in the mould. Warm the bottom of the mould in boiling water and spoon the caramel over the custard.

# Muffins & Scones

Muffins and scones are two immensely popular varieties of quick bread. For many at UBC, a scone or muffin with a hot cup of coffee is a daily ritual.

Muffins and scones lend themselves well to endless variations. Few home bakers can resist the temptation to modify and add ingredients to old recipes, often ending up with marvellous innovations. Here we present some of our most popular recipes.

# Apple Streusel Muffins

*We thank the Vancouver Sun for the original recipe.*

| BATTER | | |
|---|---|---|
| 2 cups | all purpose flour | 500 mL |
| 1 cup | granulated sugar | 250 mL |
| 1 tbsp | baking powder | 15 mL |
| 1 1/4 tsp | ground cinnamon | 6 mL |
| 1/2 tsp | salt | 2 mL |
| 1/2 tsp | baking soda | 2 mL |
| 2 | large eggs, beaten | 2 |
| 1 cup | sour cream | 250 mL |
| 1/4 cup | butter, melted | 50 mL |
| 1 cup | finely diced, unpeeled apple | 250 mL |

| STREUSEL TOPPING | | |
|---|---|---|
| 1/4 cup | granulated sugar | 50 mL |
| 3 tbsp | flour | 50 mL |
| 1/4 tsp | ground cinnamon | 1 mL |
| 2 tbsp | cold butter | 30 mL |

1. Preheat oven to 400°F (200°C). Grease 12 large muffin cups.
2. In a large bowl stir together the following ingredients: flour, sugar, baking powder, cinnamon, salt and baking soda.
3. In a small bowl thoroughly combine eggs, sour cream and butter. Add all at once to dry ingredients with apple.
4. Stir until moistened and divide batter evenly among the greased muffin cups.
5. For the streusel topping, combine sugar, flour and cinnamon. Cut in butter until mixture forms coarse crumbs.
6. Sprinkle each muffin with streusel topping.
7. Bake approximately 20 to 25 minutes.

# Blueberry Muffins

*This is the classic fruit muffin.*

| | | |
|---|---|---|
| 1 1/2 cups | all-purpose flour | 375 mL |
| 1/2 cup | sugar | 125 mL |
| 2 1/2 tsp | baking powder | 12 mL |
| 1/4 tsp | salt | 1 mL |
| 1 | egg | 1 |
| 3/4 cup | milk | 175 mL |
| 1/3 cup | melted butter | 75 mL |
| 1 cup | blueberries (fresh or frozen) | 250 mL |
| 2 tbsp | lemon rind | 30 mL |
| 4 tbsp | sugar | 60 mL |

1. Preheat oven to 400°F (200°C). Grease 12 medium muffin tins.

2. In a mixing bowl, sift or mix together flour, sugar, baking powder and salt. Set aside.

3. In small bowl, beat egg. Add milk and melted butter.

4. Add liquid ingredients to dry ingredients all at once; stir just until moistened.

5. Mix blueberries with lemon rind and sugar and stir into muffin mixture.

6. Spoon into muffin tins (about 3/4 full).

7. Top muffins with lemon rind and sugar.

8. Bake for 20 minutes.

# Carrot Muffins

*This is by far the favourite muffin on the UBC campus. Moist and delicious, not to mention nutritious.*

| | | |
|---|---|---|
| 4 | eggs | 4 |
| 1 cup | sugar | 250 mL |
| 3 cups | whole wheat flour | 700 mL |
| 2 1/2 tsp | baking powder | 12 mL |
| 1 1/2 tsp | baking soda | 7 mL |
| 1/2 tsp | salt | 2 mL |
| 2 tsp | cinnamon | 10 mL |
| 1 tsp | nutmeg | 5 mL |
| 1 cup | vegetable oil | 250 mL |
| 1 – 10 oz. | tin crushed pineapple | 300 mL |
| 2 1/2 cups | carrots, shredded | 625 mL |
| 1 cup | chopped dates | 250 mL |

1. Preheat oven to 350°F (180°C). Grease 18 muffin tins.
2. Cream eggs and sugar. Set aside.
3. Mix flour, baking powder, baking soda, salt, cinnamon and nutmeg together.
4. Add dry ingredients and vegetable oil alternately to egg/sugar mixture.
5. Add pineapple, carrot, and chopped dates.
6. Spoon into greased muffin tins.
7. Bake for 30 minutes.

# Christmas Mincemeat Muffins

*A moist fruity muffin well suited to the season. It is great for using leftover mincemeat.*

| | | |
|---|---|---|
| 1 | large egg | 1 |
| 1 tbsp | grated orange rind | 15 mL |
| 1/4 cup | vegetable oil | 50 mL |
| 1/2 cup | mincemeat | 125 mL |
| 3/4 cup | apple juice | 175 mL |
| 1 3/4 cups | all-purpose flour | 425 mL |
| 1/4 cup | sugar | 50 mL |
| 4 tsp | baking powder | 20 mL |
| 1/2 tsp | salt | 2 mL |

1. Preheat oven to 400°F (200°C). Grease 12 muffin tins.
2. Beat egg lightly with a fork. Stir in orange rind, oil, mincemeat and apple juice.
3. Combine flour, sugar, baking powder and salt. Mix into first mixture, stirring just to blend.
4. Fill greased muffin tins and bake about 15 to 20 minutes or until top springs back when touched lightly.

# Lemon Poppyseed Muffins

*A very popular tasty muffin with the crunch of poppy seeds.*

| | | |
|---|---|---|
| 2 tbsp | grated lemon rind | 30 mL |
| 1 tbsp | lemon extract | 15 mL |
| 3 cups | all-purpose flour | 750 mL |
| 3/4 tsp | baking soda | 3 mL |
| 1/2 tsp | baking powder | 2 mL |
| 1/2 tsp | salt | 2 mL |
| 1 cup | margarine | 250 mL |
| 2 cups | sugar | 500 mL |
| 4 | eggs | 4 |
| 1 cup | buttermilk | 250 mL |
| 1/4 cup | poppy seeds | 125 mL |

1. Preheat oven to 350°F (180°C). Grease 18 muffin tins.
2. Mix lemon rind and extract. Set aside.
3. Sift together dry ingredients.
4. Cream margarine and sugar.
5. Mix in eggs.
6. Add dry ingredients and buttermilk.
7. Add lemon rind, extract and poppy seeds.
8. Spoon into muffin tins and bake for 25 to 30 minutes.

# Oatmeal Date Muffins

*A excellent muffin with the goodness of oatmeal.*

| | | |
|---|---|---|
| 1 cup | oatmeal | 250 mL |
| 1 cup | buttermilk | 250 mL |
| 1 cup | flour | 250 mL |
| 1 tsp | baking powder | 5 mL |
| 1/2 tsp | baking soda | 2 mL |
| 1/2 tsp | salt | 2 mL |
| 1 | egg, beaten | 1 |
| 4 tbsp | melted butter | 60 mL |
| 1/2 cup | finely chopped dates | 125 mL |
| | rind of 1 orange | |
| 3/4 cup | brown sugar | 175 mL |

1. Preheat oven to 400°F (200°C). Grease 12 muffin tins.
2. Let oatmeal stand for 10 minutes in buttermilk.
3. Combine flour, baking powder, soda, salt and brown sugar.
4. Add eggs and butter, mixing well.
5. Pour in buttermilk mixture, adding dates and peel.
6. Spoon into muffin tins and bake for 20 minutes.

# Orange Chocolate Chip Muffins

*Orange and chocolate make a classic combination.*

| | | |
|---|---|---|
| 1 | whole orange, quartered, peeled and seeded | 1 |
| 1/2 cup | orange juice | 125 mL |
| 1 | egg | 1 |
| 1/2 cup | oil | 125 mL |
| 1 1/2 cups | flour | 375 mL |
| 1 tsp | baking soda | 5 mL |
| 1 tsp | baking powder | 5 mL |
| 1/2 tsp | salt | 2 mL |
| 1/2 cup | sugar | 125 mL |
| 1/2 cup | chocolate chips | 125 mL |

1. Preheat oven to 400°F (200°C). Grease 12 muffin tins.
2. Chop oranges finely (use blender, if desired).
3. Add egg, oil and orange juice to chopped orange.
4. Sift dry ingredients into a bowl.
5. Pour orange mixture into dry ingredients and stir lightly (adding chocolate chips), just until moistened.
6. Spoon into muffin tins and bake for approximately 15 minutes.

# Orange Cranberry Muffins

*Try these muffins at Christmas or anytime.*

| | | |
|---|---|---|
| 2 cups | cranberries, fresh or frozen, coarsely chopped | 500 mL |
| 1/3 cup | sugar | 75 mL |
| 1 tbsp | orange rind | 15 mL |
| 1/3 cup | orange juice | 75 mL |
| 2 cups | flour | 500 mL |
| 1 tsp | baking powder | 5 mL |
| 1/2 tsp | baking soda | 2 mL |
| 1/2 tsp | salt | 2 mL |
| 1/2 cup | margarine | 125 mL |
| 1 cup | sugar | 250 mL |
| 1 | egg | 1 |

1. Preheat oven to 375°F (190°C). Lightly grease 18 muffin tins.

2. Combine cranberries, 1/3 cup (75 mL) sugar, orange rind and juice. Set aside.

3. Mix dry ingredients together. Set aside.

4. Cream margarine, one cup (250 mL) sugar and egg in large bowl.

5. Add cranberry mixture and dry ingredients. Mix until just blended.

6. Spoon into muffin tins and bake for 20 minutes.

# Pina Colada Muffins

*Muffins with a touch of Mexico.*

| | | |
|---|---|---|
| 1/2 cup | sugar | 125 mL |
| 1 | egg | 1 |
| 1/4 cup | butter | 50 mL |
| 1 cup | sour cream | 250 mL |
| 1 tsp | rum extract | 5 mL |
| 1 1/2 cups | all-purpose flour | 375 mL |
| 1 tsp | baking powder | 5 mL |
| 1/2 tsp | baking soda | 2 mL |
| 1/2 tsp | salt | 2 mL |
| 1 cup | drained, crushed pineapple | 250 mL |
| 1/2 cup | coconut, medium shred | 125 mL |

1. Preheat oven to 375°F (190°C). Grease 8 – 10 muffin tins.
2. Measure sugar, egg, butter, sour cream and rum extract. Combine and beat until blended.
3. Stir together flour, baking powder, baking soda and salt; add to mixture stirring until barely blended.
4. Add pineapple and coconut. Mix.
5. Spoon into greased muffin tins and bake for about 20 minutes.

# Pineapple Zucchini Muffins

*Use this recipe when your zucchini crop gets out of hand.*

| | | |
|---|---|---|
| 3 | eggs | 3 |
| 1 1/2 cups | sugar | 75 mL |
| 1 cup | salad oil | 250 mL |
| 2 tsp | vanilla | 10 mL |
| 1 3/4 cups | unpeeled, grated raw zucchini | 425 mL |
| 10 oz. can | crushed pineapple, drained | 300 mL |
| 1 cup | chopped nuts (optional) | 250 mL |
| 3 cups | sifted all-purpose flour | 750 mL |
| 1 tsp | salt | 5 mL |
| 1 tsp | baking soda | 5 mL |
| 1/4 tsp | baking powder | 1 mL |
| 1 1/2 tsp | cinnamon | 7 mL |
| 3/4 tsp | nutmeg | 3 mL |

1. Preheat oven to 400°F (200°C). Grease 18 muffin tins.
2. Beat eggs until light and fluffy.
3. Add sugar, beating a few minutes longer.
4. Stir in oil, vanilla, zucchini, pineapple and nuts.
5. Sift together dry ingredients.
6. Add zucchini/pineapple mixture to dry ingredients. Stir just until moistened.
7. Spoon into greased muffin tins and bake for 20 minutes.

# Rhubarb Muffins

*A delectable muffin with fresh, tart rhubarb.*

| | | |
|---|---|---|
| 1/2 cup | sour cream | 125 mL |
| 1/4 cup | vegetable oil | 50 mL |
| 1 large | egg | 1 |
| 1 1/3 cups | flour | 325 mL |
| 1 cup | diced rhubarb, fresh or frozen | 250 mL |
| 2/3 cup | brown sugar | 150 mL |
| 1/2 tsp | baking soda | 2 mL |
| 1/4 tsp | salt | 1 mL |
| 1 tsp | almond extract | 4 mL |

1. Preheat oven to 350°F (180°C). Grease 12 large muffin tins.

2. Blend together sour cream, oil and egg. Set aside.

3. In another bowl, stir remaining ingredients together and combine with first mixture. Mix just until moistened.

4. Fill muffin tins 2/3 full.

5. Bake for 25 to 30 minutes.

# Rise 'n' Shine Muffins

*One of the most requested recipes from the UBC Bakeshop. It has an ensemble of ingredients, each playing an integral role in making this muffin a resounding success.*

| | | |
|---|---|---|
| 2 cups | all-purpose flour | 500 mL |
| 1 1/4 cups | sugar | 300 mL |
| 2 tsp | baking soda | 10 mL |
| 2 tsp | ground cinnamon | 10 mL |
| 1/2 tsp | salt | 2 mL |
| 2 cups | grated carrot | 500 mL |
| 1/2 cup | raisins | 125 mL |
| 1/2 cup | chopped walnuts | 125 mL |
| 1/2 cup | medium shred coconut | 125 mL |
| 2 cups | chopped apple | 500 mL |
| 3 | large eggs | 3 |
| 1 cup | vegetable oil | 250 mL |
| 2 tsp | vanilla extract | 10 mL |

1. Preheat oven to 350°F (180°C). Grease 18 muffin tins.
2. In a large bowl, combine flour, sugar, baking soda, cinnamon and salt.
3. Stir in grated carrot, raisins, walnuts, coconut and apple.
4. In another bowl beat together eggs, oil and vanilla. Stir into flour mixture until batter is just combined.
5. Spoon into well-greased muffin cups, filling to the top.
6. Bake for about 25 minutes.

# Cheese Scones

*Our most popular scone, it has been served daily at UBC for as long as the old-timers here can remember. For best results, be sure the cheese is really nippy.*

| | | |
|---|---|---|
| **3 cups** | **all-purpose flour** | **750 mL** |
| **1/2 cup** | **sugar** | **125 mL** |
| **5 tsp** | **baking powder** | **25 mL** |
| **1/2 tsp** | **salt** | **2 mL** |
| **3/4 cup** | **butter/margarine** | **175 mL** |
| **1** | **egg, slightly beaten** | **1** |
| **1 cup** | **milk** | **250 mL** |
| **1 cup** | **grated aged cheddar cheese** | **250 mL** |

**1.** Preheat oven to 450°F (230°C).

**2.** In a large bowl, mix together dry ingredients.

**3.** Cut in margarine to resemble coarse oatmeal.

**4.** Add milk and cheese to slightly beaten egg and stir into dry ingredients.

**5.** Place dough on a floured surface and knead lightly (about 12 times). Pat dough into desired thickness and cut with a 2 inch (5 cm) cookie cutter.

**6.** Place on a greased cookie sheet and bake for 15 minutes or until lightly browned.

Makes 14 scones.

# Fruit Scones

*This recipe gives an opportunity to add one cup of any fresh or dried fruit you have available.*

| | | |
|---|---|---|
| 3 cups | all-purpose flour | 750 mL |
| 1/2 cup | sugar | 125 mL |
| 5 tsp | baking powder | 25 mL |
| 1/2 tsp | salt | 2 mL |
| 3/4 cup | butter | 175 mL |
| 1 | egg, slightly beaten | 1 |
| 1 cup | milk | 250 mL |
| 1 cup | fruit (raisins, blueberries, cranberries, raspberries, mixed fruit, etc.) | 250 mL |

1. Preheat oven to 450°F (230°C).
2. In a large bowl, mix together dry ingredients.
3. Cut in butter to resemble coarse oatmeal.
4. Add milk and fruit to slightly beaten egg; stir into dry ingredients.
5. Place dough on a floured surface and knead lightly (about 12 times). Pat dough into desired thickness and cut with a 2 inch (5 cm) cookie cutter.
6. Place on a greased cookie sheet and bake for 15 minutes or until lightly browned.

Makes 14 scones.

# Ginger Raisin Scones

*For a delightful change, add this spicy scone to your baking repertoire.*

| | | |
|---|---|---|
| 2 cups | all-purpose flour | 500 mL |
| 1/3 cup | packed dark brown sugar | 75 mL |
| 1 tbsp | baking powder | 15 mL |
| 3/4 tsp | cinnamon | 3 mL |
| 1/2 tsp | ground ginger | 2 mL |
| 1/8 tsp | ground cloves | .5 mL |
| 6 tbsp | chilled butter, cut into pieces | 90 mL |
| 1/4 cup | milk | 50 mL |
| 1 | large egg | 1 |
| 3 tbsp | light unsulfured molasses | 45 mL |
| 1 tsp | vanilla extract | 5 mL |
| 2/3 cup | raisins | 150 mL |

1. Preheat oven to 375°F (190°C).
2. Grease a baking sheet.
3. Sift the first six ingredients together in a bowl.
4. Cut butter into the mixture with a pastry blender until it has the texture of coarse meal.
5. In a separate bowl, beat the egg, milk, molasses and vanilla.
6. Add the flour mixture and raisins. Stir gently until a dough forms. Form the dough into a ball.
7. On a lightly floured surface, pat until dough is one inch thick.
8. Cut dough into eight wedges and bake about 25 minutes or until a toothpick inserted in the centre comes out clean.

# Cinnamon Snails

*This is really a variation of a scone. The UBC bakers are so accustomed to making cinnamon buns, that the habit took over and the result was cinnamon snails.*

| | | |
|---|---|---|
| 3 cups | all-purpose flour | 750 mL |
| 1/2 cup | sugar | 125 mL |
| 5 tsp | baking powder | 25 mL |
| 1/2 tsp | salt | 2 mL |
| 3/4 cup | margarine or butter | 175 mL |
| 2 | large eggs, divided | 2 |
| 1 cup | milk | 250 mL |
| 6 tbsp | sugar | 90 mL |
| 1 1/2 tsp | ground cinnamon | 7 mL |

1. Preheat oven to 350°F (180°C)

2. In a large bowl combine flour, 1/2 cup (125 mL) sugar, baking powder and salt.

3. Cut in margarine or butter to resemble coarse oatmeal.

4. Beat one egg slightly and mix with milk. Stir into dry ingredients.

5. Lightly gather dough into a ball. Do not overhandle.

6. Place dough on a lightly floured surface and gently knead about 12 times. Roll out dough to 9" x 18" (22 x 45 cm) rectangle.

7. Beat remaining egg and brush over the dough. Combine the 6 tbsp (90 mL) sugar and cinnamon and sprinkle over the dough.

8. Roll up like a jelly roll, starting from the long end. Cut into 18 slices.

9. Place each slice in a paper lined muffin cup and bake for about 25 to 30 minutes.

# Apricot Pecan Scones

*Serve these warm with butter and honey.*

| | | |
|---|---|---|
| 1 cup | all-purpose flour | 250 mL |
| 1 cup | whole-wheat pastry flour | 250 mL |
| 1 tbsp | baking powder | 15 mL |
| 6 tbsp | sugar | 90 mL |
| 6 tbsp | butter | 90 mL |
| 1/2 cup | dried apricots, coarsely chopped | 125 mL |
| 1/2 cup | pecans, chopped | 125 mL |
| 2 | eggs | 2 |
| 1/4 cup | half-and-half cream | 50 mL |

1. Preheat oven to 375°F (190°C).
2. Combine in a bowl the flours, baking powder and sugar.
3. Cut in butter to resemble coarse oatmeal. Add apricots and pecans.
4. Beat eggs and cream together. Stir into the flour mixture.
5. Gather the dough into a ball and place onto a floured surface. Knead lightly (about 12 times). Pat dough into desired thickness and cut with a 2 inch (5 cm) cookie cutter.
6. Place on a greased cookie sheet and bake for 12 to 15 minutes or until lightly browned.

Makes 8 to 14 scones.

# Pies, Tortes & Flans

Here is but a small sample of the many great pies we have produced over the years. We include a flan, a cheesecake and two tortes which are often similar to pies.

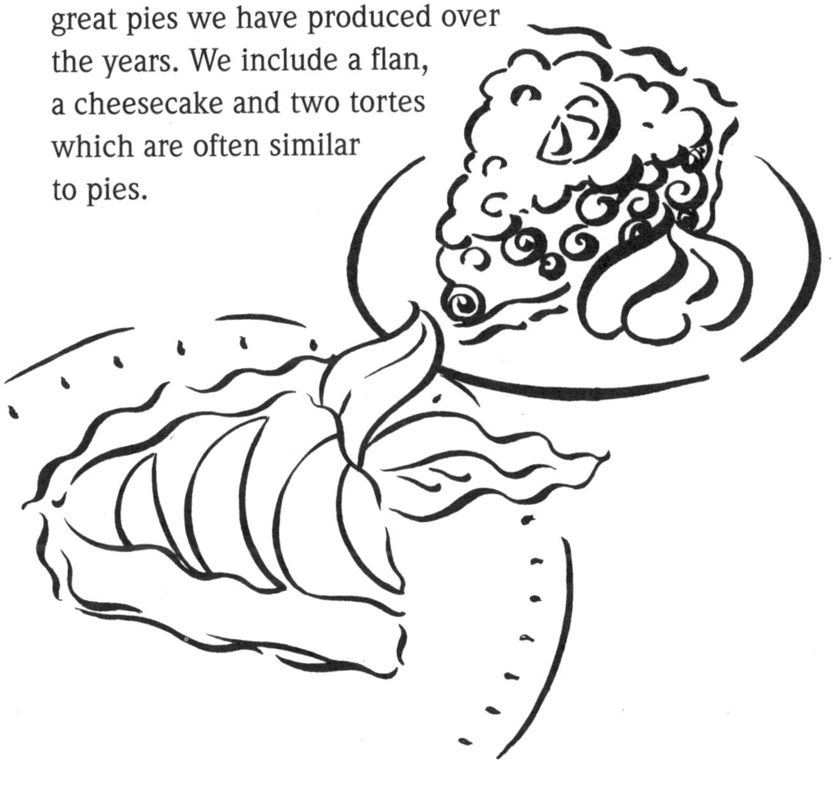

# Basic Pie Dough

*Use this dough for recipes requiring a single-crust 9 inch (22 cm) pie shell. For a two-crust pie, double the recipe.*

| | | |
|---|---|---|
| 1 cup | all-purpose flour | 250 mL |
| 1/2 tsp | salt | 2 mL |
| 1/3 cup | shortening | 75 mL |
| 1 tbsp | chilled butter | 15 mL |
| 2 tbsp | cold water | 30 mL |

1. Sift the flour and salt into a bowl.

2. Cut in the shortening and butter with two knives, a pastry blender or lightly with your fingers until the particles are about the size of small peas.

3. Sprinkle with the cold water and mix lightly with a fork until the dough thoroughly moistened and holds together. Do not overhandle. Add more water if necessary, but a very little at a time.

4. Gather the dough into a ball, cover and thoroughly chill in the refrigerator.

5. Press the dough into the approximate shape and roll it out lightly and as little as possible into a circle.

6. Put the dough into the bottom of a 9 inch (22 cm) pie pan and trim the edges with a knife. The unbaked crust is now ready for your recipe.

7. If the recipe calls for a baked crust, prick the dough with a fork, line it with wax paper and fill it with a cup of rice or beans to prevent it from puffing. Bake in a 450°F oven (230°C) for about 15 minutes or until the shell is golden.

# French Lemon Pie

*This tasty tart treat is simpler to make than Lemon Meringue Pie, but just as good.*

| | | |
|---|---|---|
| 4 | eggs | 4 |
| 1 cup | light corn syrup | 250 mL |
| 1 tsp | grated lemon peel | 5 mL |
| 1/3 cup | lemon juice | 75 mL |
| 2 tbsp | melted butter | 30 mL |
| 1/2 cup | sugar | 125 mL |
| 2 tbsp | flour | 30 mL |
| 1 | unbaked 9" pie shell | 22 cm |
| 1/2 cup | whipping cream | 125 mL |

1. Preheat oven to 350°F (180°C).
2. In a medium bowl, beat eggs well; add corn syrup, lemon peel, lemon juice and melted butter.
3. Combine sugar and flour, then stir into egg mixture.
4. Pour into unbaked pastry shell and bake for 50 minutes. Chill.
5. To serve, whip cream and mound onto pie.

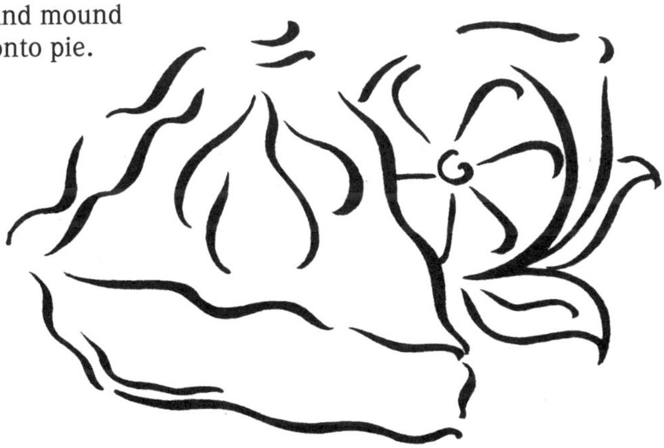

# Coffee Crème Torte

*For those who are able to plan well in advance and have storage room in their refrigerators for one week, this rich torte is well worth the wait.*

**MERINGUE**

| | | |
|---|---|---|
| **6** | **egg whites** | **6** |
| **1 1/2 cups** | **sugar** | **375 mL** |
| **1 1/2 cups** | **toasted finely ground almonds** | **375 mL** |

**FILLING & FROSTING**

| | | |
|---|---|---|
| **6** | **egg yolks** | **6** |
| **1 1/2 cups** | **sugar** | **375 mL** |
| **1/2 cup** | **strong coffee (cool)** | **125 mL** |
| **2 tsp** | **vanilla** | **10 mL** |
| **1 cup** | **soft butter** | **250 mL** |
| **1 cup** | **sliced almonds** | **250 mL** |

**MERINGUE**

1. Preheat oven to 325°F (160°C). Grease well three 8 inch (20 cm) cake pans (square or round). Line bottom with waxed paper.

2. Beat egg whites until frothy. Very gradually beat in the sugar and continue beating until stiff peaks form.

3. Fold in the toasted ground almonds.

4. Divide among prepared pans and spread evenly.

5. Bake for 50 minutes. Cool for 10 minutes, remove from pans, peel off paper and cool completely.

**FILLING AND FROSTING**

6. Beat egg yolks until light. Gradually add the sugar. Then add coffee and vanilla.

*continued...*

## Coffee Crème Torte

7. Cook over a double boiler over medium heat, stirring constantly until smooth and thickened. Cool, stirring occasionally.

8. Cream butter, add cooled custard a little at a time, beating well after each addition.

**TO ASSEMBLE**

9. Put meringue layers together using approximately a third of the filling between layers. Frost tops and sides of the torte with remaining two-thirds of the filling.

10. Place in refrigerator for about one hour so that the icing hardens enough to be wrapped well. Use tooth picks and plastic to wrap.

11. Store in the refrigerator approximately one week before serving.

12. On the day of service, toast the sliced almonds, cool and press into the cake.

Makes about 16 servings.

# Peach Flan

*Use luscious sweet peaches in season and dollop generously with whipped cream for a sensual sensation.*

| | | |
|---|---|---|
| **CRUST** | | |
| **1/2 cup** | **butter** | **125 mL** |
| **1/4 cup** | **icing sugar** | **50 mL** |
| **1 cup** | **flour** | **250 mL** |
| **FILLING** | | |
| **2 tbsp** | **peach or apricot jam, melted** | **30 mL** |
| **4 oz.** | **cream cheese** | **120 g** |
| **1 tsp** | **grated orange rind or vanilla** | **5 mL** |
| **1/2 cup** | **whipping cream** | |
| **4 – 6** | **peaches** | **4 – 6** |
| **1 cup** | **sugar** | **250 mL** |
| **3 1/2 tbsp** | **cornstarch** | **50 mL** |
| **3 tbsp** | **peach gelatin powder** | **45 mL** |
| **1 cup** | **boiling water** | **250 mL** |

**CRUST**

**1.** Preheat oven to 350°F (180°C).

**2.** Combine butter, icing sugar and flour with a pastry blender or food processor until mixture just holds together when pressed with fingers.

**3.** Pat into a 9 or 10 inch (22 or 25 cm) flan pan or pie plate or even a 12 inch (30 cm) pan. The larger the pan, the thinner the crust. Prick all over with a fork.

**4.** Bake for 15 to 20 minutes or until lightly browned. Cool.

**5.** Brush crust with melted jam to seal.

*continued...*

# Peach Flan

### FILLING

6. Beat together cream cheese, vanilla and whipping cream.

7. Spread over the jam glazed crust.

8. Arrange peach slices on top.

9. Combine sugar, cornstarch and mix well. Add slowly to the boiling water, stirring well. Cook until thick and clear. Add the 3 tbsp (45 mL) peach gelatin powder and stir.

10. Spread the mixture over the peaches. Garnish with whipped cream if desired.

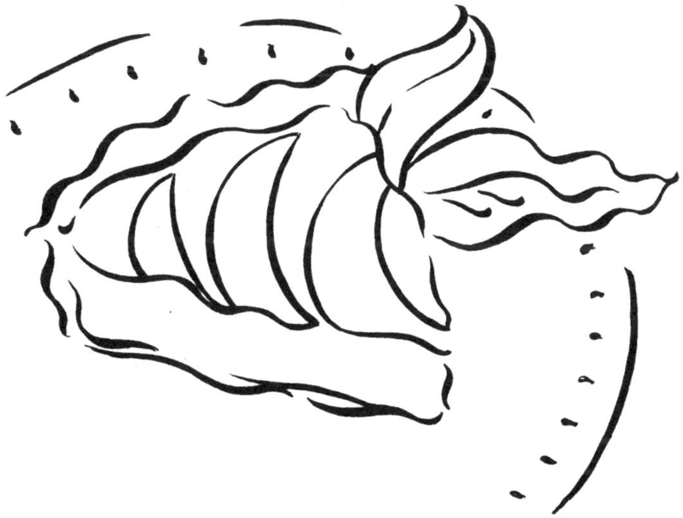

# Sour Cream Lime Torte

*Bring in a taste of the tropics with this pie.*

**CRUST**

| | | |
|---|---|---|
| 1 1/2 cups | graham cracker crumbs | 375 mL |
| 6 tbsp | melted butter | 90 mL |
| 1/2 cup | sugar | 125 mL |

**FILLING**

| | | |
|---|---|---|
| 1 cup | sugar | 250 mL |
| 3 tbsp | cornstarch | 45 mL |
| 1 cup | whipping cream | 250 mL |
| 1/3 cup | fresh lime juice | 75 mL |
| 1/4 cup | butter | 50 mL |
| 1 tbsp | finely grated lime peel (from 2 – 3 large limes) | 15 mL |
| 1 cup | sour cream | 250 mL |

**TOPPING**

| | | |
|---|---|---|
| 1 cup | whipping cream | 250 mL |
| 1/4 cup | sugar | 50 mL |
| 1 1/2 tsp | vanilla | 7 mL |
| 3/4 cup | sour cream | 175 mL |

**CRUST**

**1.** Preheat oven to 350°F (180°C).

**2.** Combine all crust ingredients in a medium bowl. Press onto bottom and sides of 9 inch (22 cm) pie pan. Freeze 15 minutes.

**3.** Bake crust until lightly browned, about 12 to 15 minutes. Cool completely on rack before filling.

*continued...*

# Sour Cream Lime Torte

**FILLING**

**4.** Mix sugar and cornstarch in medium saucepan. Gradually stir in cream, lime juice, butter and lime peel.

**5.** Bring to boil over medium-high heat, whisking constantly, then reduce heat to simmer and stir until thick and smooth, about 10 minutes. Cool to room temperature.

**6.** Fold sour cream into the cooled lime mixture. Spread evenly into the prepared crust.

**TOPPING**

**7.** Whip cream with sugar and vanilla until soft peaks form. Gently fold in the sour cream. Spread over the filling.

**8.** Chill at least 4 hours before serving

Serves 10 to 12.

# Peanut Butter and Cream Cheese Pie

*Excellent and very rich pie for peanut butter lovers.*

| | | |
|---|---|---|
| **CRUST** | | |
| **1 1/2 cups** | **graham cracker crumbs** | **375 mL** |
| **1/3 cup** | **melted butter** | **75 mL** |
| **2 tbsp** | **sugar** | **30 mL** |
| **FILLING** | | |
| **3/4 cup** | **whipping cream** | **175 mL** |
| **1 1/4 cups** | **icing sugar, divided** | **300 mL** |
| **1 tsp** | **vanilla extract** | **5 mL** |
| **1 package** | **cream cheese (250 g)** | **1 package** |
| **1 cup** | **creamy peanut butter** | **250 mL** |
| **2 tbsp** | **butter** | **30 mL** |
| **GLAZE** | | |
| **2 ounces** | **semisweet chocolate** | **60 g** |
| **2 tbsp** | **butter** | **15 mL** |

**CRUST**

1. Combine crumbs, butter and sugar. Press into bottom and up sides of a 9 inch (22 cm) pie plate. Chill in refrigerator.

**FILLING**

2. Beat whipping cream with 1/4 cup (50 mL) of the icing sugar and vanilla to form stiff peaks.

3. In another bowl, beat the remaining icing sugar, cream cheese, peanut butter and butter until fluffy.

4. Fold the whipping cream into the peanut butter mixture.

5. Spoon into the prepared crust and refrigerate about two hours or until firm.

**GLAZE**

6. Melt chocolate and butter spread over the pie. Refrigerate until the glaze is firm, about one hour.

# Sour Cream Apple Pie

*Delicious whether served piping hot or well chilled.*

FILLING & CRUST

| | | |
|---|---|---|
| 1 | unbaked, 9 inch (22 cm) pie shell | 1 |
| 1 | egg unbeaten | 1 |
| 1 cup | sour cream | 250 mL |
| 1 tsp | vanilla | 5 mL |
| 1/4 tsp | nutmeg | 1 mL |
| 3 cups | finely diced apples | 750 mL |

SPICY TOPPING

| | | |
|---|---|---|
| 1/3 cup | sugar | 75 mL |
| 1/3 cup | flour | 75 mL |
| 1 tsp | cinnamon | 5 mL |
| 1/4 cup | butter | 50 mL |

FILLING

1. Preheat oven to 400°F (200°C).
2. Beat the egg, sour cream, vanilla and nutmeg to a thin, smooth batter.
3. Stir in the apples.
4. Pour the filling into the unbaked pastry shell.
5. Bake for about 30 minutes.
6. Mix the spicy topping ingredients together.
7. Remove the partially bake pie from the oven and sprinkle on the spicy topping.
8. Bake for another 10 minutes at 400°F (200°C).

# Glazed Strawberry Pie

*Also terrific with fresh raspberries.*

| | | |
|---|---|---|
| **1 baked** | **9 inch (22 cm) pie shell** | **1** |
| **1 cup** | **strawberries (for juice)** | **250 mL** |
| **3/4 cup** | **sugar** | **175 mL** |
| **3 tbsp** | **cornstarch** | **45 mL** |
| | **pinch of salt** | |
| **2 – 3 cups** | **fresh strawberries** | **500 – 750 mL** |

1. To make juice, crush 1 cup (250 mL) of strawberries and add water to measure 1 cup. Blend the berries and water in an electric blender. Strain and add water to make up 1 cup of juice.

2. Combine and cook over low heat, stirring until thickened, the juice, sugar, cornstarch and salt over direct heat. Cool slightly.

3. Clean and hull the rest of the strawberries. Arrange evenly the remaining whole berries in the pie shell.

4. Ladle the glaze over the berries, coating thoroughly.

5. Chill in the refrigerator about 4 hours.

6. Serve topped with whipped cream.

# Fresh Blueberry Pie

*A single-crust, fresh fruit pie with blueberries accented with lemon juice.*

| | | |
|---|---|---|
| **4 cups** | **blueberries** | **1 L** |
| **3/4 cup** | **sugar** | **175 mL** |
| **3 tbsp** | **cornstarch** | **45 mL** |
| | **pinch salt** | |
| **1 cup** | **water** | **250 mL** |
| **1 tbsp** | **butter** | **15 mL** |
| **2 tbsp** | **lemon juice** | **30 mL** |
| **9 inch** | **baked pie shell** | **22 cm** |

1. In saucepan, mix 1 cup (250 mL) berries, sugar, cornstarch, salt and water.
2. Cook and stir over low heat until thick. Cool slightly.
3. Add remaining berries, butter and lemon juice. Mix well and cool.
4. Pour into baked pie shell.
5. Chill and serve with whipped cream.

# Chocolate Cheesecake Pie

*A chocolate lover's dream.*

**CRUST**

| | | |
|---|---|---|
| 1 1/2 cups | crumbs made from 6 oz. (180 g) chocolate wafers | 375 mL |
| 1/3 cup | melted butter | 75 mL |

**FILLING**

| | | |
|---|---|---|
| 6 oz. | semisweet chocolate | 180 g |
| 1 package | cream cheese (250 g), room temperature | 1 package |
| 1 tsp | vanilla | 5 mL |
| 1/2 cup | sugar, divided | 125 mL |
| 2 | medium eggs, separated | 2 |
| 1 cup | whipping cream | 250 mL |

**TOPPING**

| | | |
|---|---|---|
| 1 cup | whipping cream | 250 mL |
| 1 tsp | vanilla | 5 mL |
| 2 tbsp | icing sugar | 30 mL |

**CREAM TOPPING**

| | | |
|---|---|---|
| 1 cup | whipping cream | 250 mL |
| 1 tsp | vanilla | 5 mL |
| 2 tbsp | icing sugar | 30 mL |

**CRUST**

1. Combine crumbs with butter until well mixed. Press into a 9 inch (22 cm) pie pan and freeze crust for one hour.

*continued...*

# Chocolate Cheesecake Pie

**FILLING**

2. Melt chocolate in the top of a double boiler over boiling water. Remove from heat and set aside.

3. Beat cream cheese until smooth with an electric beater. Beat in vanilla and 1/4 cup (50 mL) of the sugar. Beat in yolks one at a time, then beat in melted chocolate, keeping the mixture smooth.

4. Beat egg whites until soft peaks form. Gradually beat in the remaining 1/4 cup (50 mL) sugar and beat until firm, but not dry.

5. Whip the cream until firm, but not stiff. Fold into the chocolate.

6. Fold the egg whites into the chocolate and whipped cream mixture.

7. Pour the pie filling into the crust, mounding it high in the centre. Chill thoroughly, preferably 12 hours or overnight.

**CREAM TOPPING**

8. Beat the whipping cream, vanilla and icing sugar together until soft peaks form. Spread over the top of the chilled pie.

# Super Delectable Apple Pie

*Truly a "Super" pie with a spiced crust, apple filling and a spiced nut crumble topping.*

| | | |
|---|---|---|
| **CRUST** | | |
| 1 3/4 cups | flour | 425 mL |
| 1/4 cup | sugar | 50 mL |
| 1 tsp | cinnamon | 5 mL |
| 1/4 tsp | nutmeg | 1 mL |
| 1/2 tsp | salt | 2 mL |
| 1/2 cup | butter | 125 mL |
| 2 tbsp | shortening | 30 mL |
| 1/4 cup | apple juice | 50 mL |
| **FILLING** | | |
| 8 | cooking apples, peeled, cored and sliced | 8 |
| 1 2/3 cups | sour cream | 400 mL |
| 3/4 cup | sugar | 175 mL |
| 1/3 cup | flour | 75 mL |
| 1 | egg | 1 |
| 2 tsp | vanilla | 10 mL |
| pinch | salt | pinch |
| **TOPPING** | | |
| 1 cup | chopped walnuts | 250 mL |
| 1/2 cup | flour | 125 mL |
| 1/2 cup | golden brown sugar | 125 mL |
| 1/4 cup | sugar | 50 mL |
| 1 tbsp | cinnamon | 15 mL |
| pinch | salt | pinch |
| 1/2 cup | softened butter | 125 mL |

*continued...*

# Super Delectable Apple Pie

1. Preheat oven to 450°F (230°C).

**CRUST**

2. Mix together flour, sugar, spices and salt.

3. Cut in butter and shortening.

4. Toss with apple juice and form into a ball.

5. Roll to fit a deep 10 inch (25 cm) pie plate. Form high ridge around top of pie plate. Set aside.

**FILLING**

6. Mix together apples, sour cream, sugar, flour, egg, vanilla and salt. Spoon into crust.

7. Bake for 10 minutes.

8. Reduce temperature to 350°F (180°C) and bake 40 minutes until lightly browned. Then add:

**TOPPING**

9. Mix together walnuts, flour, sugars, cinnamon and salt.

10. Cut in butter and mix well. Sprinkle topping over pie.

11. Bake 15 minutes longer.

# Quick Banana Torte

*Quick, easy to make and delicious.*

| | | |
|---|---|---|
| 1 cup | fine graham wafer crumbs | 250 mL |
| 3 tbsp | butter, melted | 45 mL |
| 1 1/3 cups (1 can) | sweetened condensed milk | 325 mL |
| 1/2 cup | lemon juice, divided | 125 mL |
| 2 | medium ripe bananas | 2 |
| 1 tbsp | sugar | 15 mL |
| 1 cup | whipping cream | 250 mL |

1. Combine graham wafer crumbs and butter. Set aside 2 tbsp (30 mL) of the mixture and press the rest into a lightly buttered 8 inch (20 cm) square pan.

2. Combine the condensed milk and 1/3 cup (75 mL) of the lemon juice. Stir together until smooth and thickened.

3. Dice the bananas and coat with the rest of the lemon juice. Add the sugar and mix. Stir into the milk mixture.

4. Whip the cream until stiff and fold into the banana and milk mixture. Pour into the pan and spread evenly. Sprinkle remaining crumbs on top.

5. Refrigerate for about 12 hours or until firm.

# Squares & Bars

Bars and squares are versatile and can be every cook's standby for sweet treats.

Here at UBC, Nanaimo Bars, Date Squares, Rice Krispie Squares and Chocolate Brownies are so popular that they are offered for sale every day. As well, our bakeshop features a special square each day. Recipes for some of the squares and bars made for special events, such as Convocation receptions, are also presented here.

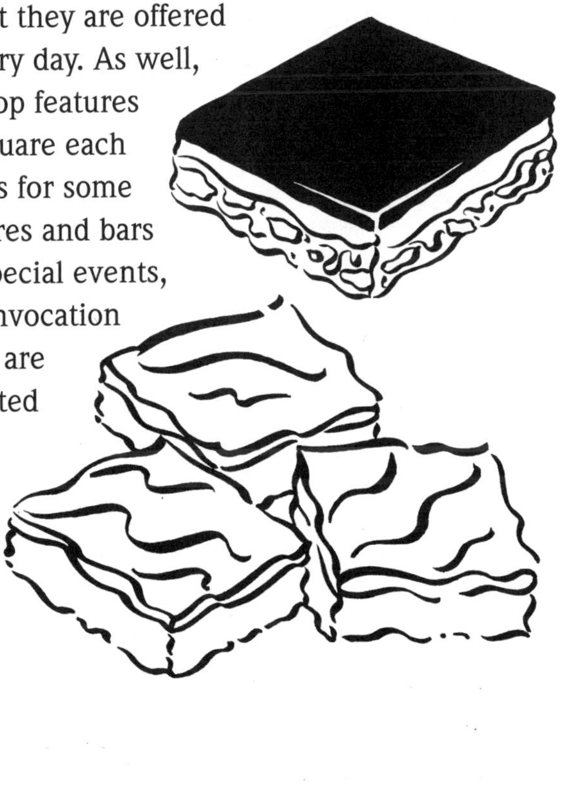

# Angie Bars

*These bars were originally called "Squamish Squares," a reflection of the popularity of "Nanaimo Bars." To avoid competition between these two west coast communities, we renamed it after Angie Jang, our Bakeshop supervisor when it was introduced.*

| | | |
|---|---|---|
| **1 cup** | **rice krispies** | **250 mL** |
| **1 cup** | **peanut butter** | **250 mL** |
| **1 cup** | **crushed cornflakes** | **250 mL** |
| **1/2 cup** | **brown sugar** | **125 mL** |
| **1/2 cup** | **corn syrup** | **125 mL** |
| **1/4 cup** | **melted butter** | **50 mL** |
| **2 tbsp** | **vanilla instant pudding powder** | **30 mL** |
| **3 tbsp** | **milk** | **45 mL** |
| **2 cups** | **icing sugar** | **500 mL** |
| **3 tbsp** | **butter** | **45 mL** |
| **3 squares** | **semi-sweet chocolate** | **3 squares** |

1. Mix rice krispies, corn flakes and peanut butter together. Stir well.

2. Combine brown sugar and corn syrup in a saucepan, heat lightly to dissolve sugar, stir and remove from heat. Mix with cereal mixture.

3. Line a 9 x 13 inch (22 x 32 cm) greased pan with this mixture and allow to chill in fridge for one hour.

4. Mix together the melted butter, vanilla pudding powder and milk. Blend in icing sugar and spread this paste over the chilled cereal layer in pan.

5. Melt the butter and chocolate squares together.

6. Stir well, then spread over vanilla custard layer.

7. Chill & cut into squares. Makes about 48 squares, 2 inches (4 cm) each.

# Lemon-Iced Apricot Squares

| | | |
|---|---|---|
| 1 cup | dried apricots | 250 mL |
| 1 cup | water | 250 mL |
| 1/2 cup | butter | 125 mL |
| 1/4 cup | sugar | 50 mL |
| 1 cup | flour | 250 mL |
| 2 | egg yolks | 2 |
| 3/4 cup | brown sugar | 175 mL |
| 1/2 cup | flour | 125 mL |
| 1/4 tsp | salt | 1 mL |
| 1/2 tsp | baking powder | 2 mL |

**ICING**

| | | |
|---|---|---|
| 1/4 cup | butter | 50 mL |
| 2 cups | icing sugar | 500 mL |
| | juice of 1 lemon | |

1. Preheat oven to 300°F (150°C).
2. Cut the apricots into very small pieces and simmer with the water for 15 minutes or until all the water is absorbed.
3. Mix the butter, sugar and flour together and press into a prepared 9 inch (22 cm) square cake pan.
4. Bake for 15 minutes. Remove the pan from the oven and increase the oven temperature to 325°F (160°C).
5. Beat two egg yolks and combine with the brown sugar, c[illegible], flour, salt, baking powder, apricots and any remaining cooking water.
6. Spread the mixture on to the crust and bake for 25 minutes. Cool.
7. Combine the icing ingredients. Spread on the cooled squares. Cut into small squares.

# Apricot Pecan Bars

*Dried apricots and pecans make this square a rich and delicious year-round treat.*

**BASE**

| | | |
|---|---|---|
| 1/2 cup | butter | 125 mL |
| 1/3 cup | firmly packed brown sugar | 75 mL |
| 1 cup | all purpose flour | 250 mL |

**TOPPING**

| | | |
|---|---|---|
| 3/4 cup | dried apricots (well packed) | 175 mL |
| 1 cup | firmly packed brown sugar | 250 mL |
| 2 | eggs | 2 |
| 1/3 cup | all-purpose flour | 75 mL |
| 1/2 tsp | baking powder | 2 mL |
| 1/4 tsp | salt | 1 mL |
| 1 tsp | grated orange rind | 1 mL |
| 1 tsp | vanilla | 2 mL |
| 1/2 cup | chopped pecans | 125 mL |
| | icing sugar | |

1. Preheat oven to 350°F (180°C). Lightly grease an 8 inch (20 cm) square cake pan.

**BASE**

2. Cream the butter, gradually adding the brown sugar and beat until light and fluffy.

3. Stir in the flour. The mixture will be quite crumbly.

4. Pat evenly into the pan.

5. Bake for 8 to 10 minutes or until light golden. Cool for 20 minutes before applying the topping.

*continued...*

# Apricot Pecan Bars

### TOPPING

6. Rinse the apricots and place in a saucepan with just enough water to cover them.

7. Bring to a boil and reduce heat and simmer uncovered for 15 minutes or until tender. Drain, cool and chop.

8. Beat the brown sugar and eggs together.

9. Sift the flour, baking powder and salt.

10. Stir the dry ingredients into the brown sugar and eggs mixture.

11. Add the orange rind, vanilla, pecans and apricots.

12. Spread over the baked layer.

13. Bake for 30 minutes or until the top is golden. Do not over bake.

14. Sprinkle the warm bars with icing sugar and cool before cutting.

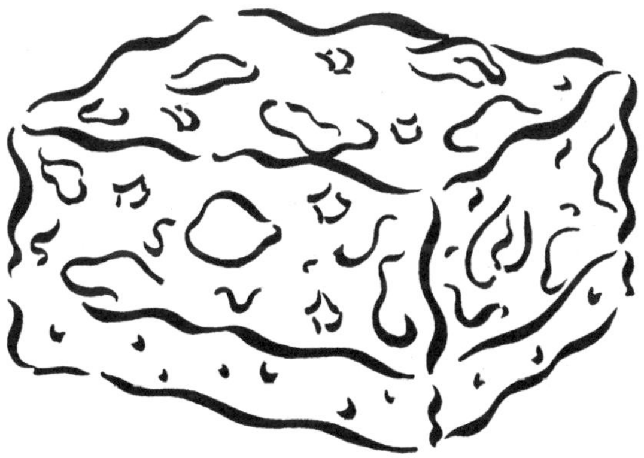

# Blueberry Bars

*Make this seasonal treat when fresh British Columbia blueberries are at their peak in late summer. The tartness of the berries is offset by the rich cream cheese icing.*

| | | |
|---|---|---|
| **1/2 lb** | **fresh blueberries** | **225 g** |
| **1 cup** | **butter** | **250 mL** |
| **1/2 cup** | **sugar** | **125 mL** |
| **1 cup** | **flour** | **250 mL** |
| **3 eggs** | **slightly beaten** | **3** |
| **1 cup** | **brown sugar** | **250 mL** |
| **1 tsp** | **vanilla extract** | **5 mL** |
| **1/2 tsp** | **flour** | **2 mL** |
| **1/2 tsp** | **salt** | **2 mL** |
| **1 cup** | **walnuts, chopped** | **250 mL** |

1. Preheat over to 350°F (180°C).
2. Rinse and drain blueberries; reserve.
3. Combine butter, sugar and flour; mix until blended. Press into a 9 x 13 inch (22 x 32 cm) pan.
4. Bake for 10 minutes or until light brown.
5. Combine eggs, brown sugar, vanilla and salt; mix until blended.
6. Dust blueberries with flour. Fold blueberries and nuts into egg mixture.
7. Pour blueberry mixture equally over crust in the 9 x 13 inch (22 x 32 cm) pan.
8. Bake for 25 minutes or until center tests done.
9. Cool and frost Blueberry Bars with cream cheese frosting.

# Butter Tart Squares

*For years, butter tarts, along with date squares, were always available at UBC. The Butter tart square has now taken the place of the butter tart. Cut this bar large or small. Let your conscience be your guide.*

| | | |
|---|---|---|
| **BASE** | | |
| 1/2 cup | margarine | 125 mL |
| 1 cup | all-purpose flour | 250 mL |
| 2 tbsp | brown sugar | 30 mL |
| **FILLING** | | |
| 2 | large eggs, beaten | 2 |
| 1 1/2 cups | brown sugar | 375 mL |
| 1/2 cup | quick-cooking oats | 125 mL |
| 1/2 tsp | baking powder | 2 mL |
| 1/4 tsp | salt | 1 mL |
| 1 tsp | vanilla | 5 mL |
| 1/2 cup | chopped walnuts | 125 mL |

**BASE**

1. Preheat oven to 350°F (180°C).

2. Cut margarine into the flour and brown sugar until crumbly.

3. Press this mixture into a buttered 9 inch (22 cm) square pan and bake for 15 minutes.

**FILLING**

4. Combine all the ingredients well and pour this mixture over the baked base.

5. Return to the oven and bake for 20 to 25 minutes. Cool before cutting into squares.

# Chewy Chocolate Peanut Bars

*Reminiscent of Almond Roca, this bar is more like candy than other bars. Thin, crisp and delicious,it's great with fresh fruit.*

**BARS**

| | | |
|---|---|---|
| 2 cups | oatmeal | 500 mL |
| 1 cup | graham wafer crumbs | 250 mL |
| 3/4 cup | brown sugar | 175 mL |
| 1/4 tsp | baking soda | 1 mL |
| 1/2 cup | salted peanuts | 125 mL |
| 1/2 cup | corn syrup | 125 mL |
| 1/2 cup | melted butter | 125 mL |
| 1 tsp | vanilla | 5 mL |

**TOPPING**

| | | |
|---|---|---|
| 1 – 6 oz | package semi-sweet chocolate chips | 170 g |
| 1/2 cup | smooth peanut butter | 125 mL |

**BARS**

1. Preheat oven to 375°F (190°C).
2. Grease a 15 x 10 inch (38 x 25 cm) pan with sides.
3. Combine oatmeal, graham crumbs, sugar, baking soda and peanuts; mix well.
4. Combine corn syrup with melted butter and vanilla. Stir into oat mixture and mix well.
5. Press firmly into pan and bake for 15 minutes.

**TOPPING**

6. Melt chocolate chips and peanut butter in a double boiler.
7. Spread over warm, baked bars and let cool 10 minutes.
8. Cut into 2 x 1 inch (5 x 2.5 cm) bars and refrigerate to set.

# Coconut Neapolitan Squares

*A coconut lover's dream come true. This square has been a favorite for many years. It is also delicious with a chocolate-peanut butter topping.*

| | | |
|---|---|---|
| **BOTTOM** | | |
| **1 1/2 cups** | **graham wafer crumbs** | **375 mL** |
| **1/2 cup** | **brown sugar** | **125 mL** |
| **1 tsp** | **baking powder** | **5 mL** |
| **1/2 cup** | **butter, melted** | **125 mL** |
| **3/4 cup** | **all-purpose flour** | **175 mL** |
| **1/2 tsp** | **salt** | **2 mL** |
| **TOPPING** | | |
| **1 1/2 cups** | **medium shredded coconut** | **375 mL** |
| **1 – 10 oz** | **tin condensed milk** | **300 mL** |
| **1 tsp** | **vanilla** | **5 mL** |

**1.** Preheat oven to 350°F (180°C).

**BOTTOM**

**2.** Combine all ingredients and pack firmly in 8 x 8 inch (20 cm ) pan.

**TOPPING**

**3.** Combine all ingredients and spread over bottom layer.

**4.** Bake for 30 to 40 minutes. DO NOT OVER BAKE. Ice with pink butter icing.

# Date Squares

*Date squares or Matrimonial Bars, as they are sometimes called, have been served at UBC since the early 1950s. They are nutritious and still a favorite for quick snacks with today's students.*

| | | |
|---|---|---|
| 1 cup | all-purpose flour | 250 mL |
| 1 tsp | baking soda | 5 mL |
| 1 cup | brown sugar | 250 mL |
| 2 cups | rolled oats (oatmeal) | 500 mL |
| 1 cup | soft butter | 250 mL |

**FILLING**

| | | |
|---|---|---|
| 2 cups | pitted & chopped dates | 500 mL |
| 1/3 cup | brown sugar | 75 mL |
| 1 1/4 cups | water | 300 mL |
| 1 tbsp | all-purpose flour | 15 mL |
| 1 tsp | vanilla | 5 mL |

1. Preheat oven to 375°F (190°C).
2. In a medium mixing bowl combine the flour, soda, 1 cup brown sugar, rolled oats and butter.
3. Rub together with fingers until it's like coarse meal.
4. Combine the Filling ingredients in a saucepan and simmer, stirring constantly until slightly thickened.
5. Press half the flour mixture into the bottom of a greased 9 x 9 inch (22 cm) cake pan.
6. Spoon filling on top and smooth with the back of a spoon.
7. Sprinkle remaining flour mixture evenly on top.
8. Bake for about 25 minutes – until top is slightly browned.

# Lemon Shortbread Bars

*These bars have the refreshing tang of lemon with a rich dough.*

**CRUST**

| | | |
|---|---|---|
| 1 cup | all-purpose flour | 250 mL |
| 1/2 cup | sugar | 125 mL |
| 1/2 cup | butter | 125 mL |

**TOPPING**

| | | |
|---|---|---|
| 1/2 cup | sugar | 125 mL |
| 2 tbsp | all-purpose flour | 30 mL |
| 1/2 tsp | baking powder | 2 mL |
| 1/4 tsp | salt | 1 mL |
| | Grated rind of 1 lemon | |
| 2 tbsp | lemon juice | 30 mL |
| 2 | large eggs | 2 |
| | icing sugar | |

**1.** Preheat oven to 350°F (180°C).

**CRUST**

**2.** Combine flour and sugar in bowl.

**3.** Cut in butter until mixture resembles fine crumbs.

**4.** Press evenly over bottom of lightly greased 8 inch (20 cm) square baking pan.

**5.** Bake for 15 minutes or until edges begin to brown. Remove from oven; cool for about 10 minutes.

**TOPPING**

**6.** Combine sugar, flour, baking powder, salt & lemon rind.

**7.** Beat together lemon juice and eggs. Stir into sugar mixture until smooth. Pour over warm crust.

**8.** Bake for 15 minutes or until top is set.

**9.** Sprinkle icing sugar over top when cool. Cut into 18 bars.

# Nanaimo Bars

*The most popular bar at UBC. This recipe is the traditional one most frequently used. However, we also serve many variations using mint, peanut butter, mocha, double chocolate and cherry fillings.*

| | | |
|---|---|---|
| **CRUST** | | |
| 2 squares | semi-sweet chocolate, melted and cooled | 2 squares |
| 2 cups | graham wafer crumbs | 500 mL |
| 1 cup | flaked coconut | 250 mL |
| 1/2 cup | softened butter | 125 mL |
| 1/2 cup | chopped walnuts | 125 mL |
| 2 tbsp | granulated sugar | 30 mL |
| 1 tsp | vanilla | 5 mL |
| 1 | egg | 1 |
| **FILLING** | | |
| 1/4 cup | softened butter | 50 mL |
| 3 tbsp | milk | 45 mL |
| 2 tbsp | powdered custard | 30 mL |
| 2 cups | icing sugar, sifted | 500 mL |
| **GLAZE** | | |
| 4 squares | semi-sweet chocolate | 4 squares |
| 1 tbsp | butter | 15 mL |

*continued...*

# Nanaimo Bars

**CRUST**

1. Combine all crust ingredients and mix well.

2. Press firmly into 9 x 9 inch (22 x 22 cm) cake pan. Refrigerate.

**FILLING**

3. Combine butter, milk and powdered custard.

4. Blend in icing sugar until smooth.

5. Spread over crust and refrigerate for at least 15 minutes.

**GLAZE**

6. Partially melt chocolate and butter over hot water.

7. Remove from heat and stir until completely melted.

8. Spread over custard layer, cover, refrigerate and cut into bars.

# Tiger Bars

*This bar, often served at special catered events, originally came from the Vancouver Sun. An easy-to-make bar enjoyed by all ages.*

**BASE**

| | | |
|---|---|---|
| 1/3 cup | butter/margarine | 75 mL |
| 1/3 cup | corn syrup | 75 mL |
| 1/3 cup | brown sugar | 75 mL |
| 1/2 cup | peanut butter chips | 125 mL |
| 2 1/2 cups | 100% bran cereal | 625 mL |
| 1/2 cup | raisins, optional | 125 mL |

**TOPPING**

| | | |
|---|---|---|
| 3/4 cup | peanut butter chips, divided | 175 mL |
| 1 cup | semi-sweet chocolate chips | 250 mL |
| 1 tsp | butter | 5 mL |

**BASE**

1. Combine butter, corn syrup and brown sugar in 2 quart (2 litre) microwaveable bowl.

2. Microwave at HIGH (full power) for two to three minutes or until mixture comes to a boil.

3. Stir in peanut butter chips, then bran and raisins.

4. Press mixture evenly into 8 inch (20 cm) square baking pan.

*continued...*

# Tiger Bars

**TOPPING**

**5.** Combine 1/2 cup (125 mL) of the peanut butter chips, the semi-sweet chocolate chips and butter in two-cup (500 mL) microwaveable measure.

**6.** Microwave at MEDIUM (half power) for 1 1/2 to 2 minutes or until chips begin melting, stirring frequently.

**7.** Spread evenly over the base layer.

**8.** Place remaining 1/4 cup (50 mL) peanut butter chips in one-cup (250 mL) microwaveable measure.

**9.** Microwave at MEDIUM (half power) for 50 to 60 seconds or until melted, stirring frequently.

**10.** Drop by teaspoonfuls over chocolate. Using a fork, swirl peanut butter and chocolate in a crisscross fashion to create stripes.

**11.** Refrigerate until firm.

# Peanut Butter Crisp Squares

*For "the kid" in all of us, a crisp square that does not require baking.*

| | | |
|---|---|---|
| **1 cup** | **peanut butter** | **250 mL** |
| **$^{1}/_{2}$ cup** | **corn syrup** | **125 mL** |
| **$^{1}/_{2}$ cup** | **brown sugar** | **125 mL** |
| **1 tsp** | **salt** | **5 mL** |
| **2 cups** | **corn flakes** | **500 mL** |
| **1 cup** | **Rice Krispies** | **250 mL** |
| **optional** | **melted chocolate** | |

1. Place sugar and syrup in double boiler. Melt.
2. Add peanut butter, corn flakes, Rice Krispies and salt.
3. Pat into 8 x 8 inch (20 cm) greased pan and refrigerate.
4. Drizzle with melted chocolate, if desired.

# UBC Granola Bars

*This recipe came to us several years ago from students in the Food Supervisory Course at Langara College. These bars provide lots of energy for long hours of study in the library.*

| | | |
|---|---|---|
| **3/4 cup** | **golden syrup** | **175 mL** |
| **3/4 cup** | **chunky peanut butter** | **175 mL** |
| **3 cups** | **5-grain granola with raisins** | **750 mL** |
| **1/2 cup** | **chopped dates** | **125 mL** |
| **1/3 cup** | **chopped dried apricots** | **75 mL** |
| **1/4 cup** | **toasted sunflower seeds** | **50 mL** |
| **1/4 cup** | **wheat germ** | **50 mL** |
| **1/4 cup** | **toasted sesame seeds** | **50 mL** |
| **1/2 tsp** | **salt** | **2 mL** |

1. Place syrup in a large bowl; microwave on full power for one minute or until boiling.

2. Add peanut butter and blend with a wooden spoon. Microwave at full power for 30 seconds.

3. In another large bowl, mix remaining ingredients. Add to hot syrup mixture and mix well.

4. Press into a greased 11 x 17 inch (28 x 43 cm) pan.

5. Cover. Refrigerate. Cut into bars and serve.

# Pecan Bars

*A favorite at our Christmas Bakeshop as well as throughout the year.*

| | | |
|---|---|---|
| 2/3 cup | icing sugar | 150 mL |
| 2 cups | all purpose flour | 500 mL |
| 1 cup | butter | 250 mL |
| 2/3 cup | melted butter | 150 mL |
| 1/2 cup | liquid honey | 125 mL |
| 3 tbsp | whipping cream | 45 mL |
| 2 cups | pecans | 500 mL |
| 1/2 cup | brown sugar | 125 mL |

1. Preheat oven to 350°F (180°C).
2. To make the base, mix together icing sugar, flour and butter.
3. Pat in a 9 x 13 inch (22 x 33 cm) pan.
4. Bake for 15 minutes.
5. Combine melted butter, liquid honey, whipping cream, brown sugar and pecans.
6. Pour the pecan mixture onto the base and smooth.
7. Bake an additional 20 minutes.
8. Cut into bars.

# Recipe Acknowledgments

We thank the following people for contributing their recipes to the UBC Bakeshop:

| | |
|---|---|
| **Zoe Afaganis** | Anise Biscotti |
| **Judy Aspol** | Pecan Bars |
| **Betty Braidwood** | UBC Coffee Cake |
| **Cathy Burton** | Over-the-Moon Rhubarb Cake |
| **Evie Cottingham** | Pineapple Cheesecake |
| **Lois Cumming** | Never Fail Chocolate Cake |
| **Audrey Davis** | Fresh Peach Cobbler |
| | Pineapple Zucchini Muffins |
| **Becky Dawson** | Super Delectable Apple Pie |
| **Sandra Dunmore** | English Christmas Pudding |
| **Linda Harris** | Trekkers Gingerbread |
| **Gail Heuchert** | Fresh Blueberry Pie |
| **Mary Jenkins** | Angie Bars |
| | Grenoble Walnut Tart |
| | Orange Chocolate Chip Muffins |
| | Traditional Scottish Shortbread |
| **Grace Ledrew** | Boiled Dark Fruit Cake |
| **Shirley Louie** | Angel's Cloud |
| | Blueberry and Lemon Mousse |
| **Irene Mayrs** | Coffee Crème Torte |
| | Fruit Cocktail Dessert Cake |
| **Gwen Nellis** | Danish Almond Shortbread |
| | Dutch Squares |
| **Ruth Philips** | Peach Flan |
| **Olga Rumen** | Carrot Muffins |
| **Jean Taylor** | Almond Crescents |
| | Christmas Cake Cookies |
| **Sharon Twamley** | UBC Granola Bars |
| **Sophia van Norden** | Blueberry Bars |

# Index


**Cakes & Quick Breads**

Almond Brickle, *22*
Banana Oatmeal Cake, *6*
Blueberry Sour Cream Cake, *8*
Blueberry Yogurt Pound Cake, *10*
Cranberry Orange Streusel Coffee Cake, *24*
Crumb Cake, *12*
Date Oatmeal Cake, *30*
Fresh Strawberry Coffee Cake, *26*
Glazed Lemon Bread, *13*
Never Fail Chocolate Cake, *14*
Over-the-Moon Rhubarb Cake, *20*
Ponderosa Cake, *15*
Pumpkin Walnut Bread, *18*
Sour Cream and Cinnamon Coffee Cake, *23*
Spicy Banana Raisin Bread, *17*
Traditional Banana Bread, *16*
Trekkers Gingerbread, *29*
UBC Coffee Cake, *28*

**Christmas Baking**

Almond Crescents, *36*
Boiled Dark Fruitcake, *33*
Brown Sugar Shortbread, *45*
Chef Erich's Brandy Sauce, *34*
Christmas Cake Cookies, *37*
Christmas Cherry Bars, *39*
Christmas Stollen, *47*
Danish Almond Shortbread, *43*
Dutch Squares, *41*
English Christmas Pudding, *32*
English Toffee, *38*
Rolled Oats Shortbread, *44*
Traditional Scottish Shortbread, *45*
UBC Hard Sauce, *35*
UBC Whipped Shortbread, *46*
Vanilla Custard Sauce, *35*

**Cookies**

Almond Apricot Biscotti, *52*
Anise Biscotti, *54*
Gingersnaps, *58*
Orange and Cinnamon Biscotti, *56*
Sugar Cookies, *50*
UBC Gourmet Cookies, *51*

**Desserts**

Angel's Cloud, *75*
Apple Betty, *60*
Blueberry Apple Crisp, *62*
Blueberry and Lemon Mousse, *63*
Cinnamon Apple Dumplings, *66*
Cranberry Cake with Hot Caramel Sauce, *64*
Crème Caramel, *79*
Fresh Peach Cobbler, *68*
Fruit Cocktail Dessert Cake, *61*
Grenoble Walnut Tart, *69*
Hot Apple Cake with Caramel Sauce, *71*
Old-Fashioned Rice and Raisin Pudding, *73*
Peach Bread Pudding, *74*
Pineapple Cheesecake, *76*
Pineapple Delight, *77*
Rhubarb Crisp, *78*

## Muffins & Scones

Apple Streusel Muffins, *82*
Apricot Pecan Scones, *98*
Blueberry Muffins, *83*
Carrot Muffins, *84*
Cheese Scones, *94*
Christmas Mincemeat Muffins, *85*
Cinnamon Snails, *97*
Fruit Scones, *95*
Gingerbread Raisin Scones, *96*
Lemon Poppyseed Muffins, *86*
Oatmeal Date Muffins, *87*
Orange Chocolate
Chip Muffins, *88*
Orange Cranberry Muffins, *89*
Pina Colada Muffins, *90*
Pineapple Zucchini Muffins, *91*
Rhubarb Muffins, *92*
Rise'n'Shine Muffins, *93*

## Pies, Tortes & Flans

Basic Pie Dough, *100*
Chocolate Cheesecake Pie, *112*
Coffee Crème Torte, *102*
French Lemon Pie, *101*
Fresh Blueberry Pie, *111*
Glazed Strawberry Pie, *110*
Peach Flan, *104*
Peanut Butter and
Cream Cheese Pie, *108*
Quick Banana Torte, *116*
Sour Cream Apple Pie, *109*
Sour Cream Lime Torte, *106*
Super Delectable Apple Pie, *114*

## Squares & Bars

Angie Bars, *118*
Apricot Pecan Bars, *120*
Blueberry Bars, *122*
Butter Tart Squares, *123*
Chewy Chocolate Peanut Bars, *124*
Coconut Neapolitan Squares, *125*
Date Squares, *126*
Lemon-Iced Apricot Squares, *119*
Lemon Shortbread Bars, *127*
Nanaimo Bars, *128*
Peanut Butter Crisp Squares, *132*
Pecan Bars, *134*
Tiger Bars, *130*
UBC Granola Bars, *133*

## UBC Cinnamon Bun, *2*

**The Editors**

Christine Samson has been the Director of the UBC Food Group since 1977. In her food service career and travels, she has avidly collected recipes from around the world. Many recipes from her collection have been adopted by the UBC Bakeshop and are included in this book.

Allen Leong is the Administration Manager of the UBC Food Group. After years of receiving public inquiries and subsequently having to read out Bakeshop recipes over the phone, he decided to initiate and coordinate the publication of *Treats To Remember.*

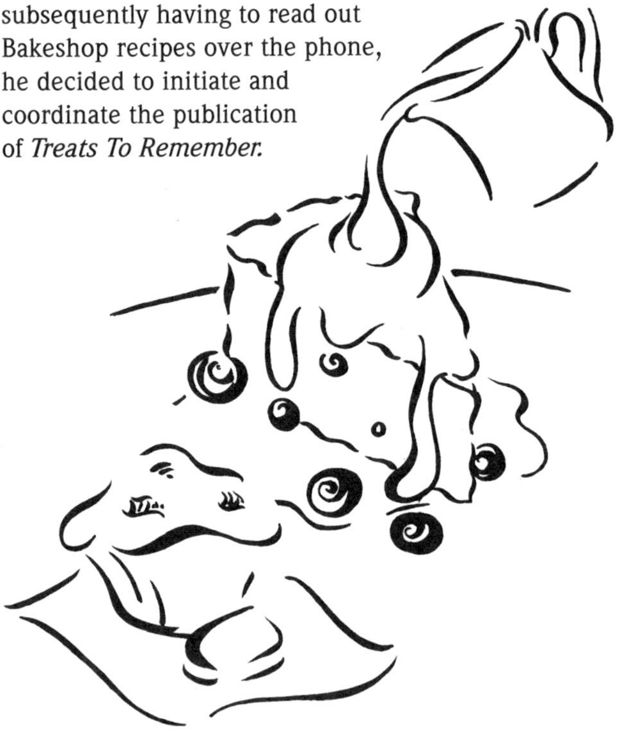